What others are saying about this book:

"IDEA is a sales company staffed by sales people. For me, the financial management chapter alone was worth many times the price of the book."
> Arnold Levin, President
> International Data Equipment & Accessories, Inc.
> Sunnyvale, California

"No contractor should be without *BIG PROFITS FROM SMALL COMPANIES*. Elements from every chapter can be used every day in my business."
> Monte Upshaw, President
> Fidelity Roof Company
> Oakland, California

"*BIG PROFITS FROM SMALL COMPANIES* presents basic concepts clearly, then builds on these concepts to derive new approaches to common problems. It is an *extremely* useful book."
> Clayton Klein, President
> Plan & Review Associates
> Los Altos, California

"Most business books are written to read from cover to cover or as a reference guide. *BIG PROFITS FROM SMALL COMPANIES* serves equally well in either capacity."
> Harold Foraker, President
> Terminal Sales Corp.
> Fremont, California

"Implementing even one of the ideas in *BIG PROFITS FROM SMALL COMPANIES* can bring thousands of additional dollars to the bottom line."
> Edward Canepa, General Manager
> El Cerrito Lighting, Inc.
> El Cerrito, California

BIG PROFITS
FROM
SMALL COMPANIES
A Manager's Guide

Steven D. Popell

First Edition

Lomas Publishing Co.
Mountain View, California

BIG PROFITS FROM SMALL COMPANIES

A Manager's Guide
by
Steven D. Popell

Published by:
    Lomas Publishing Co.
    625 Ellis Street, Suite 301
    Mountain View, CA 94043 USA

Copyright © 1985 Lomas Publishing Company

First Printing 1985
Second Printing 1985
Printed in the United States of America

Cataloging Data
    Popell, Steven D. 1939 –
    Big Profits From Small Companies

Index Information
    1. Business   2. Small Companies
    3. Management   I. Title

Library of Congress Catalog Card Number 84-52647
ISBN 0-932485-45-6 Softcover
ISBN 0-932485-44-8 Hardcover

ACKNOWLEDGEMENTS

The author gratefully acknowledges the help and support received from the dozens of individuals who contributed so generously to this project. Manuscript critics, typists, proofreaders and others have measurably improved the quality of the final product.

Most of all, deepest gratitude to my family for supporting me in this challenging undertaking and for helping me to keep it all in perspective.

WARNING – DISCLAIMER

This book is designed to provide information and suggestions on subjects related to small company management. It is sold with the understanding that neither publisher nor author is engaged in providing legal or accounting services. If such services are required, they should be obtained from a competent professional.

Reading this book is no guarantee of success. A successful manager must have a fundamental competence in his or her area of expertise, that knowledge upon which the business is to be built. The top manager must further be able to attract and keep good people, a faculty which is exceptionally difficult to teach or to learn.

Every effort has been made to keep this book free from error. However, there may be mistakes, both typographical and in content. Therefore, the book should be used as a general guide to the subjects covered, and not as the ultimate source on small company management.

Neither the author nor Lomas Publishing Co. shall assume liability or responsibility to any person or entity with respect to any loss or damage caused or alleged to be caused directly or indirectly by the information contained in this book.

If you do not agree with the above, you may return this book for a full refund.

WARNING – DISCLAIMER

For Catherine, Lauren and David

TABLE OF CONTENTS

TABLE OF CONTENTS

Table of Exhibits and Illustrations

Page

Page

INTRODUCTION

INTRODUCTION

The purpose of this book is to help you become a better manager of your small company. Every year, thousands of companies with annual sales under $10 million go bankrupt or are forced to merge with larger companies in order to survive. In many cases, either fate could have been avoided had management implemented a few or, perhaps, even one of the business practices discussed in the following chapters.

Make no mistake about it. These failures are hardly confined to restaurants and "mom-and-pop" operations. Quite the contrary, many are companies in sophisticated industries, peopled by bright, well-educated managers. These small company managers tend to be at least as competent, intelligent and attentive as their big business cousins. Unfortunately for many of them, however, their experience often cannot keep pace with their other fine qualities.

It is important to note at the outset that sophistication is of relatively little importance in successful management of a small company. The practices and techniques recommended here are primarily the "blocking and tackling" of business management. They are logical, uncomplicated, and (designed to be) easy to understand. Nevertheless, adherence to these fundamental principles can often spell the difference between success and failure.

Chapter 1 is an overview of small company management. It begins with a discussion of the causes of business failure, and includes introductory sections on marketing, finance and profitability. Chapters 2, 3, and 4 discuss, in turn, these three major management areas. Chapter 5 provides insight into the dynamic small company banking relationship and how to make the most of it. Chapter 6 discusses the practical aspects of credit and collection, and guides the reader from the establishment of important credit policies to improved collection of accounts receivable. Chapter 7 provides advice on identifying and working with outside professionals. A detailed discussion of valuing small companies and professional firms is presented in Chapter 8, and augmented with case studies in Appendices A and B. A Final Thought offers a perspective on small company management in the context of one's personal life.

It is the author's objective that this book be genuinely useful to the small company manager. Very little in these pages could be described as complex or fancy, nor do the suggestions contained herein provide a "magic formula" for small company success. They can, however, improve your company's chances for survival and prosperity.

1

SUCCESSFUL SMALL COMPANY MANAGEMENT: OVERVIEW

Why Small Companies Fail
- ❑ Functional Area Inexperience
- ❑ Functional Area Neglect
- ❑ Lack of Direction
- ❑ Inability to Anticipate Trouble

Marketing
- ❑ The Customer
- ❑ Market Dynamics
- ❑ Over-Concentration

Finance
- ❑ Credit and Collection
- ❑ Accounts Payable
- ❑ Debt Management

Profit
- ❑ Gross Margin
- ❑ Break-Even Point
- ❑ Inventory Control
- ❑ Information Management

SUCCESSFUL SMALL COMPANY MANAGEMENT: OVERVIEW

Why Small Companies Fail

Every company, large or small, has certain major categories of activity, typically referred to as functional areas. The most common of these are marketing, finance, production, engineering and administration. Most entrepreneurs will have a high level of skill and experience in their particular area of technical expertise. In fact, their reputation and successful track record in their technical area is frequently the primary motivation for starting their own business in the first place. Few, however, start out with much understanding of other important functional areas, such as marketing and finance. In such companies, there is a continual risk of turning a fertile field into a mine field.

Functional Area Inexperience

One of the most common misconceptions about small business failures is that they almost always occur as a result of poor sales. Certainly, if you don't do the business, you can't make a profit.

financial house in good order, such a cash flow

pattern can jeopardize the company's very exis-

tence. It is, therefore, of the highest importance to

make certain that your company is adequately fi-

nanced to support operations until such time as the

collection of accounts receivable (projected on a

Figure 1
Cash Flow Dynamics

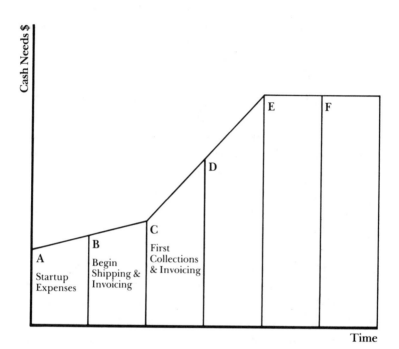

conservative basis) is sufficient to do the job.* Cash flow projection will be discussed in detail in Chapter 3, Financial Management.

Even a successful company with good cash flow can founder as a result of financial over-extension. Inexperienced management often finds it hard to protect against failure when all they have known is success. When flushed with such success, and the plaudits that go along with it, many managers will find almost irresistible the temptation to pursue market share and new markets at a pace which sorely strains financial resources. While some will get away with this strategy, many small company managers are simply unequal to the task of assessing risk versus reward in (for them) uncharted waters. Such managers would do well to take a conservative approach, so as to ensure the survival of the company even if certain projects fail.

Another common functional blind spot relates to marketing planning. Small company managers will frequently bring a product or service to the marketplace without a clear idea, let alone confirmation, that there exists a genuine market need for that product or service. This is a recipe for failure.

Even where this important first step has been taken, managers will often drastically underestimate the lead time necessary to develop sufficient sales and revenue from this product or service even to begin generating a return on investment. If the

---

*Often, a "respite" from fast growth, illustrated by line EFG, will ease financial pressure by allowing collections to catch up with new sales.

company itself is very young, the problem is compounded. To see why, simply put yourself in the position of the buyer.

If a salesperson comes to you with a new product or service, to be supplied by a relatively new company, you must get past two major roadblocks before you will be ready to write a significant purchase order. First, you must be persuaded that the new product or service will be both useful and cost effective for your company. Second, you must feel confident that this new company will be around for the foreseeable future to support its customers and provide follow-on products or services. If you were a buyer confronted with such a risk/opportunity, what would you do?

Clearly, you would approach it with extreme caution and, if and when you determined to take advantage of the opportunity, you would quite likely minimize the risk by placing only a small test order. Only under the most unusual circumstances would a knowledgeable buyer commit substantial resources to a new product or service from a relatively new company. During this period of company and product or service introduction, the strain on financial resources can be excruciating.

Here we see a prime example of the relationship between marketing and financial considerations. A relatively long lead time for producing sizeable purchase orders inevitably means an even longer delay in generating significant operating cash flow from the collection of receivables associated with those purchase orders. What that, in turn, means is that you must be sufficiently capitalized to start with, and must maintain a manageable over-head during this difficult initial phase. As simple as these two fundamental financial concepts appear to be, they are among the most ignored by aggressive small company marketeers.

Functional Area Neglect

During periods of difficulty or expansion, it is common for management to neglect one or more functional areas while addressing major problems and opportunities. Remember, the squeaky wheel isn't always the first one to fall off the wagon. Regardless of whatever else is going on, the small company manager must *always* collect accounts receivable, direct the sales force, maintain good relations with important suppliers, keep the cost of goods sold down, etc. In other words, regardless of how well or how poorly things are going at a particular time, you must attend to the basics of small company management. It is all too easy for even the most earnest manager to become distracted by the latest "fire" or "rainbow". This temptation must be resisted.

Lack of Direction

Virtually every consulting client of this firm over the last 15 years has, at one time or another, become so buried in the daily details that the big picture was lost completely. The problem of "losing the forest for the trees" is particularly prevalent in small companies because there is typically no reliable, independent sounding board within the organization. Surprisingly, even in those companies founded by two or three people, the top manager tends to dominate and, as the company grows and develops, the other founders defer more and more to that individual. The dangers and penalties associated with losing the overview of company operations in such an environment are significant indeed.

Inability To Anticipate Trouble

Early in my career, I was convinced that the intensive case method education I had received would prepare me to approach almost any business problem effectively. The absurd vanity of that delusion became apparent only over an extended period of time, during which I was forced to learn a most cruel truth; namely, that there is a seemingly endless list of small company management ideas which are perfectly logical but untrue, and an equally long list of notions which are eminently illogical but true. In addition, the makeup of these lists varies not only from industry to industry, but from company to company.

Unless you have actually been around the track, unless you have experienced some of these things before, it is very unlikely that you will see them coming. This is a very serious problem, which does not relate to intelligence, aggressiveness, hard work or the earnestness with which one attempts to pursue good management policies. Just as real estate has its three L's (Location, Location, Location), small company management has its three E's (Experience, Experience, Experience). Without it, even the brightest and most industrious manager is bound to falter.*

The ultimate result of all the above is often the exhaustion and demoralization of management. Fortunately, there are concrete steps which the aware small company manager can take to head off this kind of trouble before it becomes serious. Some general concepts in marketing, finance and profitability offered in the next three sections will provide the foundation for a more detailed discussion in the following chapters.

Marketing

Everything in business emanates from marketing. The most fundamental business questions all are marketing questions: What kind of company are we? What kind of company do we want to become? What is the "driving force" of this company; that is, what is the element that distinguishes us from competition and fuels our growth? "Leading-edge" technology? Manufacturing efficiency? Market control? Sales personnel? Accurate and far-sighted answers to these all-too-infrequently-asked questions will provide management with a solid base upon which to build a successful marketing program.

If a market does not exist or cannot be reached profitably, it doesn't matter at all how good or cheap or cost effective the product or service is. It will fail. The single most fundamental concept in

---

*It is no accident that the venture capital community almost invariably invests more readily (or at terms more favorable to the company) where the top manager has a track record of successful small company management.

marketing (small companies or large) is this: Find a need and fill it. The countryside is littered with the bodies of companies whose managements created a product or service, and only then attempted to identify and reach a viable marketplace. The small business environment is forgiving of certain kinds of management errors. This one is not among them.

The Customer

Who are the prospective customers? What are the profiles of the important customer categories? How do they buy; that is, what are their priorities among quality, price, delivery, service, etc.? Solid information on these key areas will not sell your products or services, but without such analysis, management is most likely engaging in marketing by guesswork.

Not infrequently, the nature of the customer group will be more important than the product line itself in determining important elements of marketing strategy. For example, if your company manufactures computer products which can be sold to both computer stores and industrial end users, your pricing/margin options will likely be very different. Typically, the computer stores will be reselling products which are relatively undifferentiated from those of their retail competitors. Hence, price is of the utmost importance. Industrial end users, while maintaining a keen interest in price, are equally concerned with service and delivery. In other words, the end user is typically looking for a cost-effective solution to a problem, while the computer store owner seeks to maximize resale margins on quasi-commodities.

The resulting substantial differences in margins to the manufacturer (or distributor) can have a significant impact on other aspects of the marketing program. You may be forced to pay sharply lower commissions to your sales force for computer store sales. Likewise, it may be necessary to reduce the size of your store sales force, and conduct a far greater proportion of sales over the telephone. To the extent that this strategy proves feasible, you may be able to expand your geographical territory for store sales through "phone power." Media advertising and/or direct mail may also play a much greater role than with the industrial end user.

The point of all this is that, while you must know your line of products or services and must be highly competent in your technical specialty, knowing the profile and buying habits of the various customer groups is a prerequisite to successful entry into any marketplace. The only acceptable substitute for direct personal experience in the market is solid, dependable market research. And the successful marketing executive will treat all market research with a heavy dose of skepticism. Wishful thinking has no place in a marketing plan.

Market Dynamics

Know where your market is going, and be prepared with alternative courses of action if the trend is not favorable. This principle can be illustrated with the following example:

Case History

Profile
Company Type: Sub-contractor
Annual Sales: $1.2 million
Financial Status: Good
Profitability: Moderate
Union Status: Yes
Markets: Commercial and Residential

Commercial Market Position:
  Excellent; most major competition
  unionized

Residential Market Position:
  Moderate and weakening, due to growing
  non-union competition. Homeowner
  becoming increasingly difficult to deal
  with. Size of jobs decidedly smaller than
  commercial work, resulting in a higher
  percentage of overhead per job.

Analysis of this situation was complicated by the fact that residential business carried higher gross margins than commercial business, and accounts receivable were collected much more quickly. However, it was clear that the parallel trends of consumerism and non-union competition would soon render the vast majority of residential business unprofitable for this sub-contractor. Thus, the decision was made to drop residential business and, henceforth, invest full attention in the commercial field.

This decision did entail certain risks, particularly as relating to sacrificing cash flow from an area which had represented nearly one-third of the company's sales. Nevertheless, within one year, the company was operating at a higher sales and profitability level. The lesson here, then, is to know your market or markets and, if certain trends are unfavorable, have alternatives ready to implement. If you don't, the penalty for unpleasant events which might have been foreseen could be severe.

Over-Concentration

How easy it is to be seduced into taking on one or two customers who will double or triple your sales virtually overnight? Resist this temptation, if at all possible. The bankruptcy courts are full of companies that went down that route. There are two primary reasons why this is such a risky proposition.

The obvious danger of over-concentration lies in investing substantial resources in additional plant, equipment, inventory, etc. only to find that the big customer relationship does not last. There you are, stuck with enormous unused capacity and, quite likely, requirements to service the debt incurred to finance the expansion. You can lay off people, but not depreciation and debt service. Efforts to sublet unused space can run afoul of such problems as lack of broad suitability due to custom leasehold improvements or simply over-capacity of available square footage in the area, especially in a recession.

Even if the large customer does not take its business elsewhere, it may well capitalize on its position of advantage by demanding unreasonable concessions in price or other areas. If you dump them, where is the cash flow going to come from to service the debt, let alone provide a return on your investment? Clearly, this is one of the worst kinds of dilemmas which a small company manager can face.

Less obvious is the financial risk associated with the significant increase in accounts receivable. Consider, for example, the case of a company with sales of $100,000 per month and an average age of receivable of 30 days. At any one time, this company will have approximately $100,000 invested in accounts receivable. Should that company take on a new major customer, which will provide an additional $200,000 in business per month, how much does that company now have invested in accounts receivable?

$300,000, right? Wrong! The fact is you don't know how much money this company is now going to have invested in accounts receivable unless you know how quickly the company will get paid by its $200,000 per month customer. If it gets paid in, say, 90 days, its total investment in receivables will be $700,000, rather than $300,000. (See Exhibit 1.)

Such a dramatic increase in accounts receivable ($100,000 to $700,000) would place an excruciating strain on the resources of almost any small company and, as importantly, would likely be viewed as an unacceptable risk by the company's bank or other lending institution. It represents a classic example of drowning in paper prosperity.

The most important point here is not that the bank might object and refuse to lend sufficient funds to finance the increase. Rather, such an in-

Exhibit 1

Impact of Over-Concentration on Accounts Receivable

Situation	A	B	C
Sales/Month	$100,000	$300,000	$300,000
Average Age of Receivables	30 days (1 month)	30 days (1 month)	90 days (3 months)
New Receivables Generated/Month	$100,000	$300,000	$900,000
Total Investment in Receivables	$100,000 (1 month)	$300,000 (1 month)	$900,000 (3 months)

crease would likely create an unacceptable risk to the company, reflecting poor financial management. Therefore, if this kind of "opportunity" is presented in your company, you would be wise to view it with great skepticism and to embark upon such a course only after ensuring that your financial horse is in the barn with the door locked.

Finance

The previous example demonstrates again the extent to which marketing management and financial management are related in a small company. The unfortunate fact of life is that you cannot pay the landlord with net worth, accounts receivable or any other non-cash commodity. The landlord wants only cash, and the same goes for all your other suppliers. There are only three key questions with regard to small company cash management:

1. How much cash do you have?
2. How much cash will you need?
3. Where will the difference come from?

These are not difficult questions, nor does it require a Ph.D. in Economics to figure out the answers. (See discussion of cash flow projections in Chapter 3.) Nevertheless, I have been continually surprised throughout my consulting career by the unwillingness of bright, earnest small company managers to ask themselves these simple questions, as well as the ease with which so many turn a blind eye to the most likely answers. There is no substitute in a small company for effective cash control. In difficult times, a history of tight cash policies can very well mean the difference between survival and failure or, at least, between a flourishing and a deteriorating banking relationship. Like so many other aspects of financial management, effective cash control hinges not on the mastering of some "black art" but, rather, on the desire to implement a rather easily acquired skill.

Credit and Collection

Perhaps the most important aspect of cash flow for any small company is the collection of its accounts receivable. Unless the company does cash business, receivable collection is, in fact, its only operational source of cash. It is important to emphasize at the outset that effective collection of accounts receivable begins with tough credit policies, designed to minimize the granting of credit to poor risks. In other words, you'll have a lot fewer collection problems if you avoid extending credit to poor risks. If sound credit policies are in place, and implemented firmly and consistently, many collection problems will be prevented. A comprehensive overall collection policy rounds out the picture.

The hallmark of such a policy is the doctrine that consistency and firmness are more important than fairness. "Nice guys" not only finish last in collection of accounts receivable, some don't finish at all. Remember that the day any receivable goes beyond your payment terms, you have a greater right to the money than the customer. Any assertion, overt or subtle, that the customer is the offended party, simply because you are asking for your money, should be firmly rebuffed.

40

A system of progressive discipline including letters, phone calls, cutting off supply, collection agencies, law suits, etc. – all at predictable intervals – provides the framework within which accounts receivable collection can proceed in an orderly and effective fashion. (See Chapter 6, Credit and Collection.) The customer must know what will happen if and when bills are not paid. While exceptions may be granted when appropriate, they must be exceptions and not the rule, or you will soon find that whatever business you started with has turned into a finance company.

Accounts Payable

The other side of the coin, of course, is accounts payable. It is the rare small company which has not had cash flow problems at one time or another. The handling of such problems in such a way as to avoid alienating suppliers often separates the effective cash managers from the firefighters. The most important aspect of this policy is the priority treatment of key payables.

Cash flow obligations for any small company can be divided into three major categories. First are those without which the company would be out of business. These would typically include utilities, payroll taxes and single source material suppliers. Category 1 suppliers must be unique and essential for the company's continued operation. This uniqueness may relate to the quality of the product or service provided, its price or both. Clearly, it doesn't matter if you can get a similar quality product elsewhere at a prohibitively higher price or a competitively priced product that doesn't do the job. An irreplaceable supplier of such a product or service is a category 1 supplier.

Category 2 suppliers are those which would be extremely difficult or inconvenient to replace, but for which there is an adequate substitute, as well as debt service and the payroll for key personnel. Category 3 represents the rest. Which supplier, then, do we ignore?

The answer is: None! These three supplier categories must be allocated cash in accordance with their priority. But no supplier, however small, can be ignored with impunity. Remember that a small supplier can cause you almost as much grief, aggravation and financial jeopardy as a large one. In addition, fundamental precepts of ethics and common decency dictate that even the most humble be treated with courtesy and respect.

What this means in practice is that, if you do not have the cash to pay a particular supplier, it is your responsibility to contact that supplier, preferably *before* the debt is due. The substance of this (telephone) contact should be as follows:

1. Confirmation of the exact amount of debt, together with invoice numbers, associated dates and any other necessary detail.

2. Acknowledgement of the debt, and a commitment to liquidate it. It is essential that the supplier be convinced that you intend to honor your financial responsibility.

3. Explanation of the cash flow problem, in as much detail as possible without jeopardizing the company's financial reputation.

4. Proposal and agreement on a schedule of payments.

Any reader who has spent much time collecting accounts receivable will realize immediately the beauty of this approach; namely, that it will allow you to rise above, and be regarded as different from, your supplier's other collection problems. Knowing from experience that virtually no customer ever makes such a call and, quite the opposite, the vast majority waits for *you* to contact *them*, such a customer will stand out as one meriting trust. This confidence will be bolstered if the payment schedule is met. Even if this schedule is met only partially, but any shortfall is forecast by a similarly timely telephone call, that trust will likely be maintained. Such good will should enhance your company's financial reputation, rather than detract from it, and provide valuable additional time to solve your cash flow problems.

What will be the reaction of the accounts receivable collection person to such an approach? Is he or she likely to hound that company or even take great pains to implement the company's collection policy with regard to that customer? On the contrary, few, if any, collection personnel will actively pursue a customer who makes it a practice to initiate contact. They simply have too many *real* deadbeats to worry about.

Debt Management

One final note is worthwhile in this overview of financial management. Avoid taking on more debt than the company can service in bad times. Always try to leave some additional borrowing capacity for a rainy day. The concept of borrowing heavily for capital needs in order to minimize one's investment and, hence, maximize one's return on investment, is appealing, but often risky. This notion, called leverage, is illustrated in Figure 2. The circled A represents your basic big boulder, which cannot be moved with muscle strength alone. The triangle B represents a fulcrum. The long straight line C represents the lever which, in conjunction with the fulcrum, will allow the operator to move rock A. The operator is able to do this by exerting a relatively modest amount of downward pressure on that portion of the lever labeled C-1, which will transmit a rather larger amount of upward pressure on the rock from the end of that portion of the lever labeled C-2. In the financial world, C-1 is debt (somebody else's money) and C-2 is equity (your money.)

For those founders who wish to maximize their return on investment, don't wish to have their equity interest diluted by outside investors, or simply don't have a lot of money, the concept of leverage can be very tempting. Exhibit 2 will demonstrate why.

The unfortunate fact is that, while leverage is wonderful on the way up, it is terrible on the way down. And even in bad times, the debt must be

Figure 2
Leverage

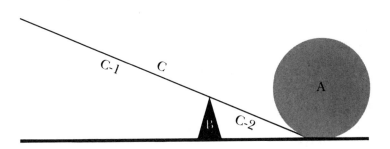

Exhibit 2

Advantages of Leverage

Assumptions:

1. Investment required: $100,000
2. Situation A: Entirely from founder
3. Situation B: One-half from bank at 15% interest per year
4. Pre-tax, pre-interest profit of $30,000
5. Taxes at 30% of income

	A	B
Investment by Founder	$100,000	$50,000
Debt from Bank	—	50,000
Pre-tax, pre-interest profit	30,000	30,000
Interest	—	7,500
Pre-tax profit	30,000	22,500
Taxes (30%)	9,000	6,750
After-tax profit	$ 21,000	$15,750
Return-On-Investment	21,000	15,750
	÷	÷
	$100,000	$50,000
	21%	31.5%

serviced, including principle and interest. It is the unwise financial manager who saddles the company with debts that it may not be able to repay in bad times.

Profit

Management analysis and utilization of the profit and loss statement will be discussed in detail in Chapter 4. Four subjects are appropriate for particular emphasis in this Overview chapter; namely, gross margin, break-even point, inventory control and information management. An in-depth understanding of these concepts will afford a very useful perspective of income statements and balance sheets.

Gross Margin

By far the most important line of the income statement (P&L) is that of gross margin (also called gross profit). Gross margin represents net sales minus the cost of goods sold. Cost of goods sold includes all costs directly related to the production of the product or provision of the services invoiced during the accounting period. If a company has a high gross margin in dollars and percent, its management can make some mistakes "below the line" and still make a profit. The company which has a poor gross margin in dollars and percent has two strikes against it immediately. Any significant mistake in general and administrative or selling expenses will seriously jeopardize profits or, quite possibly, cause a loss. While one can never underestimate the importance of keeping overhead under control, the fact remains that if you saddle yourself with poor gross margin, there is almost no chance that your company can be highly prosperous.

What constitutes a "good" or "poor" gross margin will vary from industry to industry. For example, a high technology company requires a very high gross margin (55% or more) in order to support the ongoing research and development necessary to remain technically competitive. At the other end of the spectrum, certain distributors can survive with a gross margin of 20% to 25%, if their overhead structure is low relative to sales volume. The average manufacturing company can do well with a gross margin of 50%. Learn what is typical for your industry, and set out to beat that figure by 5%.

Break-Even Point

Break-even point is defined as that level of sales which will yield neither profit nor loss, and is calculated as a function of overhead and margin. One cannot over-emphasize the importance to the small company manager of knowing what sales the company must generate, given reliable assumptions as to overhead and margin, in order to keep from losing money. Such information can be invaluable in determining, for example, the prudence of a proposed investment in additional plant and equipment or the taking on of a large customer at a greatly reduced margin.

It is clear from even a casual perusal of an income statement that there will be a direct relationship between overhead costs and break-even point. For example, a company with 50% margin will need to generate $200,000 in sales to yield $100,000 in margin. Therefore, if the company's overhead is $100,000 per month, it will have to generate $200,000 per month in sales in order to break-even. If their overhead were to double to $200,000 per month, their break-even point would also double – to $400,000 per month.

As important, but not as obvious, is the inverse relationship between margins and break-even point, assuming overhead remains the same. If, as in the above example, a company has an overhead of $100,000 per month and a 50% margin, the break-even point is $200,000 per month. If the margin drops to 25%, while the overhead remains the same, the break-even point will again double to $400,000 per month. The point here is that a substantial reduction in margin can and will destroy profit unless corresponding cuts in overhead are effected, or volume is increased dramatically without a corresponding increase in overhead, a tall order under the best of circumstances.

Inventory Control*

Inventory control is one of the most frustrating aspects of profit and financial management, primarily because of the inherently conflicting na-

---

*The reader may be wondering at this point why a subject as detail-oriented as inventory control should appear in a chapter presenting an overview of small company management. The reason is that good inventory control is typically indicative of a clear management understanding of the relationships between marketing and finance, along with a commendable attention to detail. Hence, the management that runs its inventory well generally manages the entire company well.

ture of the five factors affected by inventory control management; namely, cost of money, availability of cash, risk of obsolescence, delivery delays and end user turnover. For example, the company that maintains no finished goods or work-in-process inventory at all, but manufactures or distributes strictly to order, has no cost of money associated with carrying inventory (with the possible exception of raw materials), and the availability of cash for other uses is not affected. In addition, there is no risk of obsolescence whatever. On the other hand, there are typically significant delays in delivery and resultant customer dissatisfaction and, frequently, end user consumption and reorder are adversely affected.

Conversely, if management maintains a gigantic inventory, orders can be processed out of that inventory with minimum delay and maximum customer satisfaction, with the greatest possible chance for end user consumption and reorder. Nevertheless, inventory carrying charges are high and large amounts of cash cannot be used for other projects within the company. In addition, the risk of obsolescence is quite substantial, particularly with high technology products.

There is no "perfect" level of inventory, because any inventory level carries with it certain advantages and disadvantages for both marketing and finance. Achievement of a proper inventory balance is often indicative of an in-depth management understanding of its customers, marketplace, products and financial resources. Such an understanding is essential for successful small company management. (See Chapter 4 for a discussion of inventory control methods.)

Information Management

Underlying all aspects of profit management are the systems which provide the information on which management decisions are based. Monthly financial statements and sales reports, agings of receivables and payables, payroll records and personnel files and a host of additional categories of management information depend upon the accurate and timely collection, evaluation, summary and display of information from throughout the company. The proper operation of the information system is as important as any task on the management agenda.

Whether or not the information system, or part of it, utilizes a computer is a function of the sheer mass of information, its complexity and the extent of manipulation of raw data into different report formats or repetitive "what if" analyses. As important is the level of sophistication and computer experience not only of management, but among those who would actually operate the computer on a daily basis. (See Chapter 4.)

But whatever the systems, manual and/or computer, management *must be* thoroughly familiar with their operation, and be able to locate and process information despite illness, vacation or incompetence of subordinate operators. The manager who is totally dependent upon a subordinate for information risks not only delays and interruptions in the information flow but, as well, a filtering process which may obscure as much as it reveals.

2

MARKETING MANAGEMENT

- ❑ Analysis
- ❑ Volume
- ❑ Product or Departmental Mix
- ❑ Geography
- ❑ Direct Sales Force
- ❑ Sales Representatives
- ❑ Distributors
- ❑ Effectiveness of Advertising
- ❑ Elasticity of Demand
- ❑ Product Necessity
- ❑ Market Share
- ❑ Action
- ❑ Setting Up a Profitable Territory
- ❑ Improving Marketing's Contribution to Profit
- ❑ Account Control and Penetration
- ❑ Phasing Out Losers
- ❑ Outside Sales Personnel

MARKETING MANAGEMENT

Analysis

It is impossible to manage a marketing effort without having a clear and detailed understanding of the market situation. Such an effort requires the capacity to collect information, display it in a readable and understandable fashion, evaluate it, make decisions and implement and control those decisions. Without this capacity and the will to use it, most marketing efforts will fail.

Several items are of particular importance in analyzing the marketing situation of any small company:

1. Volume

2. Mix by product, department and/or geography

3. Sales force (direct, reps, distributors)

4. Advertising

5. Elasticity of demand

6. Product necessity

7. Market share

With regard to any and all of these factors, it is not just the static situation which must be analyzed but, more importantly, the significant trends.

Volume

If you were to ask 100 small company managers for the annual sales volume of their company, probably 99 would give you a figure like $1 million. Unfortunately, such a single piece of static information such as that is of limited value for marketing planning. Far more helpful is the trend of that volume in relation to previous periods, particularly when broken down into various important categories. Volume by product or service, geographical area, sales person, etc., and the trends in each of these categories, are the stuff from which quality marketing decisions are made. Current information in all such categories should be compared as follows:

1. This month vs. last month

2. This month vs. the same month last year

3. Year-to-date this year vs. year-to-date last year

4. Previous projections, if any

Remember, the greatest company and industry overview in the world will not keep management from making poor decisions if those decisions are based on inaccurate or inadequate information detail.

Product or Departmental Mix

Of particular importance is the product or departmental mix. Besides the self-evident desirability of tracking sales volume trends among individual products or departments, there is a less obvious, but equally important, reason for doing so. That reason is that the gross margin of different products or service departments will often vary considerably and, as a result, the product or departmental mix can have a significant impact on the overall gross margin of the company.

This principle is illustrated in Exhibit 3. Here we see that a drop from 50% to 25% of total sales of the company's higher margin product has the impact of reducing the company's overall gross margin from 50% to 45%. Assuming sales and overhead are unchanged, this margin reduction would cost a company with $1 million in annual sales about $50,000 in both gross margin and pre-tax profits. Any aspect of company operations which can so significantly affect overall gross margin must be monitored with great care.

Geography

Many small company managers view territorial information on sales volume (and margins) strictly as an indicator of geographical market preference and/or company or product line strength in particular regions. Frequently, however, it is even more indicative of the relative effectiveness of various segments of the company's sales force. This information can be important not only as an aid to

Exhibit 3

Impact of Product or Departmental Mix On Overall Company Gross Margin

Situation 1

	Margin	% of Total Sales
Product A	60%	50%
B	40%	50%

Overall company margin
50% of 60% = 30%
+ 50% of 40% = 20%
————
50%

Situation 2

	Margin	% of Total Sales
Product or Dept. A	60%	25%
B	40%	75%

Overall company margin
25% of 60% = 15%
+ 75% of 40% = 30%
————
45%

management in selecting and replacing sales personnel, but for determining the most appropriate type of sales force for any one geographical area – direct sales personnel, reps and/or distributors.

Direct Sales Force

A direct sales force is one which is on the company payroll. Management has the right to hire and fire from this sales force, as well as to have the final say in matters of compensation, fringe benefits, etc. From this relationship flows the most important advantage of the direct sales force; namely, control over the activities of the individual sales person. Your sales people are dependent upon you for feeding their families and, therefore, are much more likely to conduct themselves in the field in accordance with company policies and directives. The primary disadvantage is that you are paying them all the time, whether they are successful or not. And an unsuccessful direct sales force can be very expensive to maintain.

Sales Representatives

Sales representatives (reps) are quite different from a direct sales force, in that they run an independent business in which they sell "lines" from a number of suppliers. When they are successful in bringing in business, reps receive a commission, typically a fixed percentage of sales dollars. For the small, cash-poor company, reps can provide a low risk approach to the marketplace because, if little or no sales are produced, then little or no commissions are paid. In addition, the company does not have obligations for payroll taxes and fringe benefits which would attend a direct sales force commitment. There will be some costs associated with sales trips to rep territories, literature, telephone contact, etc. Nevertheless, the risks associated with unsuccessful selling are dramatically reduced.

The disadvantage of a rep relationship is the *lack* of control over the activities of the sales person in the field. Reps will typically devote the bulk of their time to their "bread and butter" accounts. Because they know that a growing company will often replace their field reps with direct sales people when they have the financial resources to do so, they are always on the lookout for new lines. Nevertheless, they have families to feed, and will not invest any more time in a new company or product line than can be justified by short term rewards. In addition, reps are notorious for their lack of cooperation in submitting marketing information and/or paperwork required by the company's marketing management. These problems tend to be tolerated by management, because utilization of reps will often allow the company to penetrate markets which would be inaccessible to them on a direct basis.

Distributors

For the company which wants to make quick inroads into a difficult marketplace, selling through a distributor can provide one possible solution. A distributor is an independent company which buys from the manufacturer and sells to the retailer or other end user. Primary advantages of dealing with the distributor center around that company's access to the marketplace. This access will often lend credibility to the products of a company not yet well known. It can also make feasible a sales effort to small customers, whose limited sales volume potential would render a direct sales effort unprofitable. These factors will often combine to allow a distributor to place much larger orders with a manufacturer than the company can reasonably expect to get from other sources. Such volume orders can be of great help to a small company in speeding up the manufacturing learning curve and bringing down the unit cost of production.

On the other hand, the addition of another company in the marketing stream between the manufacturer and the end user invariably cuts manufacturer margins substantially. This principle is illustrated in Exhibit 4. Clearly, there could be only two possible justifications for such a dramatic decline in unit margin in dollars and percent; first, a significant increase in sales volume with a proportionately lower increase in overhead costs; and, second, a dramatically reduced unit cost to manufacture because of such an increase in sales volume.

It is worth repeating that an analysis of sales volume by product or department and geographical territory must carefully take into consideration the type and effectiveness of the particular sales force. While sales performance in one territory might be improved by changing the product mix, another might require the improved technical competence and increased intensity of a direct sales force, and yet a third might require only a change in personnel. A continual and accurate assessment of information

Exhibit 4

Impact of Distributor Sales on Margins[1]

Situation 1

Mfr. Net Sale Price/Unit	$100
Cost of Goods Sold	40
Gross Margin	$ 60 (60% of Net Sale)

Situation 2

Mfr. Net Sale Price/Unit[1]	$ 60
Cost of Goods Sold	40
Gross Margin	$ 20 ($33\frac{1}{3}$% of Net Sale)

---

[1]Assumes distributor discount of 40%.

from the field is absolutely essential to the formulation and implementation of correct marketing decisions.

Effectiveness of Advertising

One factor which can undermine management's efforts to analyze realistically various sales volume trends is an inability to *measure* the effectiveness of its advertising program. There is an old saying that goes, "I know half my advertising budget is worthless; I just don't know which half." In most small companies, this is the rule rather than the exception.

While a detailed analysis of advertising measurement is beyond the scope of this book, it is important to stress that an effective management team *must* measure the impact of its advertising, whether that measurement takes the form of retail couponing, bingo cards, telephone surveys or something else. To invest in advertising without a clear idea of the effectiveness of that advertising not only risks wasting money but, as importantly, can compromise the accuracy of sales volume trend analysis, and the marketing decisions that flow from it. Industry statistics on the advertising budget, as a percentage of sales, can help set initial guidelines for advertising expenditures and, perhaps, give some clues as to a reasonable return on your advertising investment.

Elasticity of Demand

Demand for a product or service is said to be elastic if a relatively small change in price will generate a relatively large change in sales volume. Elastic demand will typically be found in markets in which the product or services are not easily differentiated. A market is said to be inelastic if a relatively large change in price will have little or no impact on sales volume. An inelastic market will typically be found where the products or services are easily differentiated and, in particular, where product or service quality is of utmost importance to the customer.

For example, a relatively small change in the manufacturer's price for paper clips will inevitably have a significant impact on sales volume. On the other hand, a relatively large percentage increase in the price of a component for a top-of-the-line, high-tech instrument might not affect sales volume at all. It is important that management have a firm grasp of where each of their products or services ranks in terms of elasticity of demand. Needless to say, an inelastic market will yield better margins and will generally be more stable than an elastic one. Being positioned at the high-quality end of any market is nearly always an advantage.

Product Necessity

It is also important for management to know how necessary to the user each of the company's products or services is. To the extent that any product or service is unnecessary to its customer base, it will be vulnerable to economic cycles. This is not to say that products which represent luxuries or even "frills" cannot be profitable and worthwhile vehicles for investment. What it does say is that maintaining a line of products or services which are exclusively so runs the risk of having the entire company cycled continually through boom and bust. The marketing and financial disadvantages of such instability can be quite serious.

Market Share

Of all the considerations discussed here relating to analysis of the marketing situation, market share is the least important, particularly if your sales represents a tiny portion of the total market. Indeed, there are certain distinct markets which are relatively small and, if you are a "big fish in a small pond", monitoring market share may be important for you. However, if the information is difficult to get, don't bother. In 99 cases out of 100 small companies, it is not worth the effort.

Action

Setting Up a Profitable Territory

The importance of prior experience in a market and good market research has been emphasized previously in the context of a "go or no-go" decision. Once the decision to enter a market has been made, however, these factors are of equal importance in setting up and managing a successful territory. There are two basic methods commonly used to estimate the sales potential of a particular territory, breakdown and buildup.

The breakdown method relies on available statistical data on the size of the market over some very large geographical area (world, national, regional). From these data are extrapolated the likely market size for the proposed territory. Without belaboring the obvious, it is important to note that a direct mathematical relationship (e.g. in proportion to population) is appropriate *only* where the territory closely mirrors the larger market. When this is not the case, adjustments must be made to reflect these differences, or the extrapolation will be of little use.

In all cases, and especially where breakdown data is shaky, the buildup method is of great importance. This method requires identifying specific sources of sales *within* the territory. Such data as customer lists, numbers of users, the quantity of installed equipment, etc., form the basis for this investigation. In-depth discussions with major potential customers, and/or random sample investigations of the total customer base, can help "flesh out" your analysis. Learning when a customer or customer group is likely to buy, and how much initially, is as important as their identification as bonafide potential purchasers.

Be conservative in forecasting territory sales. If there is a significant discrepancy in results between the buildup and breakdown methods, the buildup method will usually be more reliable. If the realistic potential is small to moderate, reps may be a useful approach. If that potential is moderate to large, direct people may be better in the long run, although they will cost more initially. If the territory contains many smaller or geographically remote accounts, then a distributor may be the answer — either alone or in concert with your rep(s) or direct sales force. The quality of your decisions in these matters will relate directly and uncompromisingly to the extent of your knowledge of the market.

Improving Marketing's
Contribution of Profit

I always ask a seminar audience what the primary function of the sales force is. Invariably answers come back such as:

1. Get sales.

2. Generate purchase orders.

3. Develop market information.

4. Service the customers.

5. Handle complaints.

6. Introduce new products.

Not so! In fact, the sales force has only one key task in any company, large or small, and that is to generate profit. Whatever functions the sales force performs in generating purchase orders, providing customer service or acting as a conduit for information are only means to an end. Without profit, the company and the jobs of the sales force will not long survive. Any bozo can sell a ten dollar bill for five dollars. Only an effective sales person can maximize the sales of those company products or services which have the highest margins and can help to generate the highest bottom-line profit.

One way to increase marketing's contribution to profit would be to organize a more effective mix of sales force types. We have discussed previously the advantages and disadvantages of a direct sales force, reps and distributors, as well as the importance of accurate information on the effectiveness of each type and each individual entity within that type. Armed with such information, management can decide with confidence what changes, if any, may be appropriate.

A note of caution here. It is typical for the small company to try to replace all of its reps when it has the financial resources to support a direct sales force. The reasoning is that, once a territory is established, a direct sales force may be not only more controllable, but cheaper to maintain than a commissioned force of reps. While the theory is compelling, replacement of an effective rep with an untested direct sales person simply on the basis of perceived savings may be foolhardy. There is no reason why any two or three of these sales force types cannot coexist side-by-side. Likewise, there may be little justification for replacing a small rep or distributor with a larger one, just to get more "bodies" into the territory. The key factor in all this is the effectiveness of the individuals.

Account Control and Penetration

Whatever type(s) of sales force you employ, two major objectives will be account control and account penetration. Account control refers to a relationship in which the customer feels such dependence upon the salesperson for advice and guidance, and such complete confidence in the quality of the salesperson's service, that another vendor is never seriously considered – even at a somewhat cheaper price. (Regardless of the relationship, a major price discrepancy will get any buyer's attention.) Seldom will anyone but an experienced and talented salesperson exert a high degree of account control. If you are fortunate enough to have such an individual working for you, be generous in your pay package and effusive in your praise. In short, don't lose him!

In addition to reducing the threat of low margins and/or losing the account, employing such an effective salesperson in a territory will typically increase sales by improving account penetration – the percentage of the customer's business which your company gets. This concept is, of course, of particular relevance in large companies for the obvious reason that big customers usually write bigger purchase orders than small ones. Less obvious, but as important, is the fact that large companies frequently have many divisions. A first-rate salesperson will use account control and penetration in one division as a springboard for attacking other divisions.

The one drawback to the kind of sales performance described above is that it is very time consuming and, therefore, usually incompatible with full coverage of all accounts in the territory. There are two common solutions to the problem of not enough hours in the day to reach all the accounts. First is a simple territory adjustment. (If you are the salesperson, read this as territory cutback or reduction.) This solution works well for ordinary sales personnel, and can usually be made acceptable by allowing a certain number of "hold" accounts from the lost territory, especially where the customer relationship is particularly strong, and/or a partial commission on lost accounts for several months.

For our star salesperson, this approach is far less appealing because it severs the very in-depth relationships which are the basis for key account control and penetration. A better idea is to add a second salesperson to the territory, whose assignment is to cover smaller established accounts and "smokestack" for new ones. In this way, account control and penetration are fostered without adversely affecting territory coverage.

Phasing Out Losers

Phasing out losers can also be a significant help in improving marketing's contribution to profit. Not infrequently, the sales force may object to the elimination of a product or product line which it feels is essential for the company's image in the marketplace. "It fills out the line." is frequent justification for retaining such a product. How should management deal with such objections? Broadly speaking, it has three choices. First, it can disregard these complaints altogether and yank the product or product line at will. Second, it can buckle under the pressure from the sales force and abandon the idea altogether. Third, management could raise the price. The advantage of this last approach is that, if the sales force is correct, the market will bear the additional price, and the product will begin to carry its own weight. If not, it will disappear, without the necessity of management appearing to be insensitive to the professional expertise and feelings of the sales force. Such a posture by management in its marketing decisions can make a major contribution to the maintenance of high morale among an employee group where feelings of frustration, isolation and "us versus them" are all too prevalent.

Outside Sales Personnel

The importance of taking human factors into account in making business decisions, as illustrated in the previous section, has been management dogma for decades. This concern is particularly important in dealing with outside sales personnel because of the unique profile of this particular employee group. This profile is a direct reflection of the difficulties and frustrations routinely encountered by those earning a living from outside sales.

The travail of the outside sales person only begins with the customer. Set up appointments, have them broken. Arrive for appointments only to find that the customer will not see you and didn't even give you the courtesy of canceling the appointment in advance. In the car, out of the car. Sample cases, airport parking lots, planes, hotels, most prospective customers saying no. Current customers calling you more frequently to voice complaints than to place orders. After a while all the hotel rooms are the same, and all the prime ribs are the same. And no amount of luxury can make up for the grind, not to mention the loneliness for those away from their families for extended periods of time.

Obviously, the selling profession covers a wide spectrum as to skill, knowledge, personality, character and degree of organization. Nevertheless, there are certain elements which are common to those who are successful in outside selling. Principal among these are toughness, resilience and the ability to be a self-starter, even under adverse conditions. Simply getting out of bed in the morning in a strange city after an unsuccessful previous day is, in itself, a noteworthy achievement. As well, the ability to function effectively with minimal face-to-face support from company colleagues merits the respect of management.

In fact, it is this very separation from headquarters which provides some of the greatest frustration for outside sales personnel. If you are spending a vast majority of your time on the road, the worst aspect of that life is not the broken appointments, the rude customers, the complaints, or the percentage of "No" answers from prospective or, even, current customers. Rather, the thing that really bugs you is the feeling that you are not getting proper support from the people in your own company. There you are, out on the firing line, *knowing* what's going on in the marketplace, and having to deal continually with some nincompoop back at the head office who wouldn't know a customer if he fell over one. There he is, back there in his cushy office, telling you what to do and loading you up with a bunch of paperwork to describe how well you are doing it. How does that make you feel? Isolated.

If there is one negative feeling among outside sales personnel which is more important and more troubling than any other, it is the feeling of isolation. With isolation comes alienation and, with that, the potential for an irreversible decline in morale. The sales force is the lifeblood of any company, large or small. While this group must be controlled, both in terms of action and reporting responsibility, the management which chooses to run roughshod over the opinions of outside sales personnel will do so at the company's peril.

A far better approach is actively to solicit opinions from the field on any and all matters in which field sales experience can be helpful for management, together with effective follow-up regarding decisions made. This means letting the individual know that at least some of his or her advice has been followed, and thanks for your interest and effort. "If not, why not, and thanks anyway. You are a valuable member of this team. We might not take your advice all the time, but we want the benefit of your experience and judgment all the time." (Keep those cards and letters coming, folks.)

3

Financial Management

FINANCIAL MANAGEMENT

Introduction

Small company financial management is easy. This may come as a surprise to those of you who view this management activity as mysterious and requiring an in-depth knowledge of accounting. The purpose of this chapter is to dispel any concern you might have as to your adequacy in tackling financial management in your company.

Balance Sheet Analysis

Exhibit 5 presents a sample balance sheet. It is called a balance sheet because it has to balance. Now, the balance sheet will balance simply by subtracting the liabilities from assets, and identifying the difference as net worth. If there are more assets than liabilities, the company has a positive net worth (also called equity or book value), and if liabilities exceed assets, the company has a negative net worth. A few key definitions would be helpful here.

Exhibit 5

Sample Balance Sheet

ASSETS			LIABILITIES			
Current Assets			**Current Liabilities**			
Cash	$100,000		Accounts Payable			$150,000
Marketable Securities	50,000		Accrued U.S. Income Tax			50,000
Accounts Receivable	200,000		Debt Due Within One Year			150,000
Inventory	150,000					
Total Current	$500,000		Total Current			$350,000
Fixed Assets			**Long-Term Liabilities**			
Furniture	25,000		Long-Term Debt			125,000
Equipment	75,000		Equity:			
Less Accum. Depr.	(25,000)		Capital Stock		25,000	
Net Fixed	75,000		Capital Surplus		25,000	
			Retained Earnings		50,000	
			Total Equity			100,000
TOTAL ASSETS	$575,000		**TOTAL LIABILITIES**			$575,000

78

Current Assets are those assets which either are cash or can reasonably be expected to turn into cash within one year.

Quick Assets are those assets which either are cash or can reasonably be expected to turn into cash within 90 days. Typically this will mean cash, cash equivalents (such as certificates of deposits) and accounts receivable.

Fixed Assets comprise land, buildings, and equipment less accumulated depreciation.*

Current Liabilities are those liabilities which must be paid off within one year, while long-term liabilities are due after one year.

Net Worth equals total assets minus total liabilities.

Tangible Net Worth equals tangible assets minus total liabilities.

Intangible Assets are those assets which would be difficult or impossible to sell because of their lack of general usability (e.g. highly customized computer programming) or their existence as an accounting entry only (e.g. "goodwill").

---

*There is a third category of assets; namely, Other Assets. However, this category typically represents such a tiny portion of total assets, it is not worth discussing in this context.

Retained Earnings is the total of all after-tax earnings (less dividends to stockholders) from the inception of the company to the present.

With these definitions in mind, we can get to the business of analyzing the balance sheet.*

Balance sheet analysis relies heavily on the relationship between certain asset and liability categories. For example, total assets minus total liabilities equals net worth. Current assets minus current liabilities equals working capital, a measure of the company's ability (in dollars) to handle its short-term financial obligations. Often these asset/liability relationships are expressed in ratio form. Below are the four most important:

$$1. \ \text{Current Ratio} = \frac{\text{Current Assets}}{\text{Current Liabilities}}$$

This ratio expresses the relationship between those assets which are cash or can reasonably be expected to turn into cash within one year and those liabilities which must be paid off within one year. If this ratio is less than 1:1 (more current liabilities than current assets – commonly referred to as negative working capital) the company is likely to have difficulty in discharging its 12-month obligations. A ratio of 2:1

---

*The Bank of America, *Small Business Reporter*, Vol. 14, No. 6, entitled "Understanding Financial Statements", is highly recommended for its basic introduction to this subject. Individual copies may be obtained at a cost of $2 each by writing to the Small Business Reporter, Bank of America, Dept. 3401, P.O. Box 37000, San Francisco, CA 94137.

or better typically indicates a good short-term financial condition.

2. Quick Ratio (Acid Test) =

$$\frac{\text{Cash} + \text{Cash Equivalents} + \text{Accounts Receivable}}{\text{Current Liabilities}}$$

This ratio quantifies the relationship between those assets that either are cash or can reasonably be expected to turn into cash within 90 days and the 12-month obligations. This ratio should be at least 0.65:1. 1:1 or better indicates good short-term financial condition. The logic here, of course, is that the company has sufficient liquidity to cover its 12-month debts solely from current cash and cash to be generated during the next 90 days. Owing to the importance of this measure of short-term financial health, my advice is that you never fall flat on your acid test.

3. Ratio of Equity to Long-Term Debt =

$$\frac{\text{Net Worth}}{\text{Total Debt} - \text{Current Liabilities}}$$

Long-term debt is most frequently used to finance fixed assets. This ratio provides an important indicator of additional long-term borrowing capacity. A ratio of greater than 2:1 is quite favorable and would typically indicate significant additional long-term borrowing capacity.

$$\text{4. Debt-to-Worth} = \frac{\text{Total Debt}}{\text{Tangible Net Worth}}$$

The ratio is of particular importance to bankers, because it gives a clear indication of the relative risk of investors and creditors. A high ratio of debt to worth (say, 4:1 or 5:1) will generally discourage bank lending. On the other hand, a very small ratio, such as 0.2:1, will indicate to many loan officers that the management of the company is too conservative, and is unduly restricting its expansion possibility. Freely translated, this means that if you are that good at managing the company's money, we'd like to lend you some.

The balance sheet displayed in Exhibit 5 yields the following ratios:

$$\text{Current Ratio} = \frac{\$500,000}{\$350,000} = 1.43:1$$

$$\text{Quick Ratio} = \frac{\$100,000 + \$50,000 + \$200,000}{\$350,000} = 1:1$$

$$\text{Equity to Long Term Debt} = \frac{\$100,000}{\$125,000} = 0.8:1$$

$$\text{Debt to Worth} = \frac{\$350,000 + \$75,000 + \$50,000}{\$100,000} = 4.75:1$$

It would be difficult for a company with this balance sheet to generate substantial additional borrowing. While there is considerable liquidity represented by the $350,000 in Quick Assets, total debt exceeds equity by nearly a 5:1 margin. In addition, retained earnings accumulated thus far are not impressive. Most loan officers would insist on a significant improvement in both the debt-to-worth ratio and retained earnings before considering any additional lending.

Funds Flow Analysis

The purpose of Funds Flow Analysis is to determine how money moved within a company during a certain period of time. This is extremely important financial information and is very easy to determine. Also referred to as Sources and Uses of Funds or Sources and Applications of Funds, the procedure is to determine mathematically where the money came from and where it went.

Since this analysis depends upon the categorization of sources and uses of funds, one must have an easy way to determine which is which. Put simply, a reduction of an asset or an increase of a liability is a source of funds, while an increase of an asset or a reduction of a liability is a use of funds. The logic of this system becomes apparent when one considers a few simple examples.

If management takes $50,000 from the cash account to buy a machine or pay down bank debt, then the cash account has been the source of funds. The same thinking applies to the reduction of *any other* asset account, such as Accounts Receivable. An increase of an asset, on the other hand, represents a use of funds, as in the purchase of additional equipment or an increase in the level of Accounts Receivable.

As one would expect, the liability side of the balance sheet represents the other side of the coin. For example, if management borrows $50,000 to purchase a fixed asset, bank borrowing has been the source of funds. The same concept would apply to the increase of any other liability. Contrariwise, a reduction of a liability, such as paying down accounts payable or bank debt, is a use of funds. Again, the same concept applies to the reduction of any other liability.

With these guidelines in mind, the manager need only compare two successive balance sheets, line by line, to determine which items represent sources and which, uses of funds. Exhibit 6 presents balance sheets for December 31, 1982 and 1983. Exhibit 7 shows the long form of sources and uses of funds developed from these two balance sheets, while Exhibit 7A shows the short form. Let's review just three or four specific examples.

Cash reduced from $100,000 to $40,000, thereby developing a source of funds of $60,000. Hence, an entry should be made on the Sources and Uses of Funds sheet under Sources saying 'cash $60,000'. In the same one-year period, Accounts Receivable increased by $25,000, and a corresponding entry under Uses should be made for accounts receivable. On the liability side, debt due within one year increased from $150,000 to $200,000, thereby

Exhibit 6

Funds Flow Analysis
Balance Sheet — 12/31/82

ASSETS		LIABILITIES		
Current Assets		**Current Liabilities**		
Cash	$100,000	Accounts Payable		$150,000
Marketable Securities	50,000	Accrued U.S. Income Tax		50,000
Accounts Receivable	200,000	Debt Due Within One Year		150,000
Inventory	150,000			
Total Current	$500,000	Total Current		$350,000
Fixed Assets		**Long-Term Liabilities**		
Furniture	25,000	Long-Term Debt		125,000
Equipment	75,000	Equity:		
Less Accum. Depr.	(25,000)	Capital Stock	25,000	
		Capital Surplus	25,000	
Net Fixed	75,000	Retained Earnings	50,000	
		Total Equity		100,000
TOTAL ASSETS	$575,000	**TOTAL LIABILITIES**		$575,000

Exhibit 6 (continued)

12/31/83

Current Assets			**Current Liabilities**		
Cash	$ 40,000		Accounts Payable		$150,000
Marketable Securities	50,000		Accrued U.S. Income Tax		50,000
Accounts Receivable	225,000		Debt Due Within One Year		200,000
Inventory	250,000				
Total Current		$565,000	Total Current		$400,000
Fixed Assets			**Long-Term Liabilities**		
Furniture	25,000		Long-Term Debt		225,000
Equipment	175,000		Equity:		
Less Accum. Depr.	(30,000)		Capital Stock	25,000	
			Capital Surplus	25,000	
Net Fixed		170,000	Retained Earnings	60,000	
			Total Equity		110,000
TOTAL ASSETS		$735,000	**TOTAL LIABILITIES**		$735,000

Exhibit 7

Sources and Uses of Funds
Calendar Year 1983

Long Form

SOURCES		USES	
Cash	$ 60,000	Accounts Receivable	$ 25,000
Depreciation	5,000	Inventory	100,000
Debt Due Within	50,000	Equipment	100,000
One Year			
Long-Term Debt	100,000		
Retained Earnings	10,000		
Total	$225,000	Total	$225,000

Exhibit 7A

Short Form

SOURCES		USES	
Current Liabilities	$ 50,000	Current Assets	$ 65,000
Long-Term Liabilities	100,000	Net Fixed Assets	95,000
Retained Earnings	10,000		
Total	$160,000*	Total	$160,000*

*The totals for Sources & Uses of Funds must be equal. If they are not, you may have put one account on the wrong side. Take the difference between the totals and divide by 2. If that amount is equal to any individual item, that may be the culprit. If not, you have a mathematical error or more than one misplacement and (sorry) you'll have to start again.

generating a source of funds of $50,000. Finally, depreciation is a source of funds, because funds flow analysis is concerned with the movement of cash within the company, and depreciation is a non-cash expense. Exhibit 7 is typical of funds flow analysis, in that three or four large items dominate, thus facilitating easy understanding and use.

While a thorough financial analysis of the company whose balance sheets are shown in Exhibit 6 would include much additional information, Exhibit 7 does provide some very useful insights. In a year in which the company added only $10,000 to retained earnings, it borrowed $150,000 and took $60,000 from the cash account in order to invest primarily in equipment and inventory. Absent other information to the contrary, such as credible projections of greatly increased earnings in the very near future, one could conclude that the overall financial condition of this company has deteriorated during this one year period. This tentative conclusion is supported by the fact that all key financial ratios are worse at 12/31/83 than at 12/31/82 as follows:

	'82	'83
Current Ratio	1.43:1	1.41:1
Quick Ratio	1:1	0.79:1
Equity to LTD	0.8:1	0.49:1
Debt to Worth	4.75:1	5.68:1

Funds flow analysis can be very revealing, and should be performed no less often than annually, more frequently if there is trouble.

Cash Flow Projection

When one considers how beneficial cash flow projection is for any small company's financial planning and operating performance, and how easy it is to do, it's a wonder that so few managers bother, except perhaps to satisfy the bank. Below is a brief explanation of the proper procedure for this important work.

Referring to Exhibit 8, we begin with the opening cash balance (AAA). Next is a projection of cash receipts from all sources. Accounts receivable collections represent the primary source of cash for nearly all non-retail small companies. Projecting collections requires two steps: first, projecting sales (invoices billed to customers); and, second, projecting how long it will take to collect after the date of invoice. For example, if your company projects sales as follows:

1st Qtr.	2nd Qtr.	3rd Qtr.
$200,000	$300,000	$400,000

and a collection period of 90 days, then projected collection would be:

2nd Qtr.	3rd Qtr.	4th Qtr.
$200,000	$300,000	$400,000

More accurate projections can be made from a monthly sales forecast, and most companies project cash on a monthly basis 12 months ahead. This

Exhibit 8
Cash Flow Projection Form

	1st Qtr.	2nd Qtr.	3rd Qtr.	4th Qtr.
Opening Cash Balance	AAA	BBB	CCC	DDD
Receipts				
A/R Collections				
Cash Sales				
Bank Loan				
Sale of Equity				
Other				
Total Rec.				
Disbursements				
Material				
Direct Labor				
Indirect Labor				
Rent				
Utilities				
Commissions				
Other Sell. Exp.				
Other Overhead				
Total Disb.				
Net Cash Flow For Period				
Closing Cash Balance	BBB	CCC	DDD	EEE

91

procedure is acceptable. The main concern is to avoid "rose-colored glasses" on collections. A major over-estimation here can sink a financial plan. The same comment would apply to the other Receipts line items, all of which are projected according to when the cash is actually expected to arrive.

Disbursements total all cash expenditures, and reflect *only* actual cash out of the checkbook. Depreciation and other non-cash items are excluded. Further, it makes no difference when you receive a bill or when it is due for payment – only when it is actually paid. Total disbursements for the period are subtracted from total receipts to yield net cash flow for the period. If receipts exceeded disbursements, this net figure is added to the opening cash balance to yield the closing cash balance (BBB). If disbursements exceeded receipts, this number is subtracted. The closing cash balance, of course, becomes the opening cash balance for the following period.

These calculations will help you immeasurably to identify and make provision for cash needs (seasonal, for expansion, to cover temporary losses, etc.) and to schedule supplier payments when cash is tight. They may also force consideration of economy measures *before* the need becomes acute. Neglect of this vital aspect of cash management can jeopardize the very financial health of the company.

4

PROFIT MANAGEMENT

PROFIT MANAGEMENT

Introduction

In order to manage profit, management must have a consistent monthly statement, which is both accurate and timely. "Consistent" means that the statement is constructed in the same way from month to month and year to year. "Timely" means that the statement should be delivered to management soon enough after the end of the period to allow a meaningful reaction to financial events. Usually, a statement which is ready between the 15th and 25th of the month following will satisfy this requirement.

The financial statement need not be prepared by a CPA, but must be of high quality. Who prepares the statement is far less important than the quality of the statement itself. The best arrangement is one in which the company hires its own full-charge bookkeeper (defined as an individual who is qualified to prepare both the balance sheet and the income statement.) If your company cannot afford such an individual, or cannot find one sufficiently qualified, then the statements can be prepared by an outside accountant, based upon posted accounting data prepared by lower level inside personnel.

When you receive this statement, you should compare it, line by line, with statements of the previous month, the same month in the previous year and the year-to-date statement of the previous year. Comparisons of financial ratios and line-item percentages of net sales can be very revealing as to the financial and profitability trends of the company. All unusual items, positive or negative, must be investigated thoroughly to determine origin, importance and implications for future management decisions.

Comparisons with industry data are seldom very illuminating for small companies. In fact, such data is often misleading, because so many small company managers are reluctant to release confidential information to a source over which they have no control. Consequently, most either refuse to submit such data or shade the truth in their submission. The result is often unreliable information from a small sample. If reliable industry data is at all difficult to obtain, don't waste the time trying.

Profit Analysis by Department or Product Line

Analyzing an income statement solely in the aggregate can hide problems or opportunities within specific departments or product lines. Therefore, it is important to analyze financial results broken down by these categories. This process has two steps; first, determination of gross margin and, second, allocation of expenses. In the vast majority of cases, the most fundamental cost accounting techniques are more than adequate. You need only develop judgments on each income statement line item as to the proper allocation per department or product line. For example, rent and utilities are most frequently allocated by square footage. Officers' salaries should be apportioned in accordance with the amount of time devoted to each category. Even though these judgments are frequently subjective, they are an essential part of this process and are better than no judgments at all.

The usefulness of this technique was illustrated a number of years ago by a client in the wholesale-retail tire business. This client had excellent gross margin information, broken down by category of tires (new car, new truck, used and recaps) as well as batteries and accessories, and brake and mechanical (auto repair). After allocating expenses in accordance with the best judgments which could be made at the time, it was determined that brake and mechanical, which provided 17% of sales revenue, provided 51% of pre-tax profits. Armed with this information, management made the obvious decision to pursue brake and mechanical business much more aggressively. If you know the right questions, the right answers are often self-evident.

Break-Even Calculation

This important financial calculation was discussed in Chapter 1. Our purpose here is to demonstrate the calculation, and the extent to which break-even can be affected by charges in the sales mix.

Break-even point equals fixed expenses divided by the net margin percentage. (Net margin is defined here as the gross margin percentage less the percentage of all other expenses which vary directly and proportionately with sales.) The basic calculation and an illustration of the impact of a mix change are presented in Exhibit 9. The break-even calculation should be performed no less frequently than quarterly.

But what do you do if companywide margins are slipping, and reduction of fixed expenses seems impossible or, at least, impractical?

1. Most important, remember that *gross margin is the most important line on the income statement.* Improvement in gross margin dollars and percent must remain a top management priority at all times.

2. Attempts to improve margins should begin with cost reduction. Every item of cost must be analyzed and reanalyzed to identify possible areas of improvement. Only when this process has been exhausted should management turn its attention to item 3.

3. Investigate the feasibility of selective price increases consistent with competitive conditions and market commitments.

4. Overlaying all these considerations is the effectiveness of the sales force in selling

Exhibit 9

Effect of Mix Change on Break-Even Point

Assumptions:

1. Product #1 Gross Margin 60%
2. Product #2 Gross Margin 40%
3. All other variable expenses = 10% of Net Sales
4. Fixed expenses = $50,000 per month
5. Situation A:
   Product #1 = 50% of Sales
   Product #2 = 50% of Sales
6. Situation B:
   Product #1 = 25% of Sales
   Product #2 = 75% of Sales

Situation A

Company Gross Margin =

$$50\% \text{ of } 60\% = 30\%$$
$$+ \ 50\% \text{ of } 40\% = \underline{20\%}$$

Total	50%
Less Other Variable Expenses	(10%)
Net Margin	40%

BEP =

$$\frac{\text{Fixed Expenses}}{\text{Net Margin \%}} = \frac{\$50,000/\text{mo.}}{.4} = \$125,000/\text{mo}$$

Break-Even Point = $125,000/mo. Net Sales

99

Exhibit 9 (continued)
Situation B

Company Gross Margin =

$$25\% \text{ of } 60\% = 15\%$$
$$+ 75\% \text{ of } 40\% = \underline{30\%}$$

	Total	45%
Less Other Variable Expenses		(10%)
Net Margin		35%

$$BEP = \frac{\$50,000}{.35} = \$142,847$$

Break Even Point = $142,857/mo.
  Net Sales, an increase of
  $17,857, or 14.3%

NOTE: If total company unit sales remain the same, there will be a drop in Gross Margin, Net Margin and Pre-tax Profit of 5% of Net Sales, or $6,250.

those products or services which carry the highest gross margins. It is the responsibility of management to take steps to insure that the sales force will so conduct itself in the field. In this regard, the sales compensation program can have a material impact.

Sales Compensation

To pay a salesperson a fixed percentage of sales dollars (say, 10%) on a product or service with a 60% margin, and pay the same 10% of sales for a product with 40% margin makes little sense. The notion that these two financial events are in any way equal is frivolous. As discussed in Chapter 2, the function of the sales force is to generate profit, not just write purchase orders. To base a compensation program solely on sales dollars is to give the sales force the incentive to generate sales, not profit. For the management which wants to do something other than eat soup with a fork, this distinction is critical. Far preferable is a compensation system which rewards high performance in gross margin dollars and percent. An example of such a program is presented in Exhibit 10.

There are infinite variations of this basic concept. The important point is not the exact makeup of the program but the fact that the sales force is rewarded for its contribution to gross margin and, thus, has a real incentive to conduct itself in such a manner as to help maximize company profitability. Any sales compensation program which makes money for only sales person OR company (but not both) is a recipe for failure.

Exhibit 10

Sales Compensation
Based Upon Gross Margin

Gross Margin %	% of GM $ to Salesperson
15–19.9%	15%
20–24.9	20
25–29.9	25
30–34.9	30
35–39.9	35
40 and up	40

Example: Salesperson generates $50,000 sales in a month, with an aggregate Gross Margin of 30% ($15,000). Commission calculation as follows:

$$\$15,000 \text{ x } 30\%^{[1]} = \$4,500$$

Sales Commission For Month	= $4,500

[1]Representing the salesperson's share of the Gross Margin $ at a GM % of 30–34.9%

Additional Thoughts on Gross Margins

Management must always keep in mind that the margins on old products or services are probably eroding. In some cases it may not be possible to raise their prices any more. Therefore, the margins on new products and services must be kept up or, otherwise, company-wide margins will drop. It will almost always be easier to keep labor and material costs down in a depressed economy, because the law of supply and demand will be working in your favor. But whatever the economic conditions or the demands of your suppliers or labor force, you must maintain adequate margins to cover your overhead and generate a significant bottom line profit or the whole reason for your being in business in the first place will have been undermined.

Inventory Control: A Word on Methods

There are many methods of controlling inventory, both manual and automated, but all depend upon two basic elements; first, an accurate and detailed periodic physical inventory; and, second, the input and processing of all inventory-related events, including orders placed with suppliers and estimated delivery dates, merchandise received from suppliers, orders received from customers, merchandise shipped to customers, and the most recent physical inventory itself. If the input of inventory event information is accurate and timely, the output for management use is merely a function of simple mathematics. With any decent manual or automated system, you will know quickly how soon you can fill an order for a customer, and which items will probably have to be reordered soon from suppliers. Likewise, you can derive your total inventory investment and turnover rate. Unfortunately, all this is a far cry from effective inventory control. For this, we must get deeply into the details.

There is an old saying about the stock market that says it isn't really a stock market, but rather a market of stocks. Meaning: The movement of the Dow may or may not be relevant to the specific stock(s) you hold at any particular time. Similarly, only careful analysis of the sales (and margins) of specific items and product categories will be of genuine help in making specific purchasing decisions. The key questions are these:

1. What is the sales history of each product and product line?
2. What seasonal factors are involved in this history?
3. What is the turnover rate of key product lines or categories?
4. How low can you allow the stock of each product to get without undue risk of stock-out and possible loss of an order (reorder point?)
5. How much should you reorder (reorder quantity) when the stock reaches the reorder point or drops below it?
6. What products or lines can be eliminated, thereby giving you greater buying power with the equivalents you retain?
7. What products have the best margins?
8. What can you do to increase the turnover of high-margin products? (Yes, this is a sales

management question, but one with important implications for inventory control. For example, if a substantial portion of the market will pay a premium for immediate delivery of a high-margin product, avoidance of a stockout in that product would be an important objective; hence, a heavy inventory investment would usually be justified, unless, perhaps, the product has a significant risk of obsolescence with little warning).

The list can go on, but the concept is more important. If you want to exercise effective control over your inventory, get down into the trenches and learn the details. Know what moved this month and this year-to-date. Compare this performance with last month, and with this month last year and last year-to-date. Plot seasonality and product maturity; and from all this, develop your reorder points and quantities. Drop lines, flex your muscles with suppliers. Go for price concessions and extra freight allowances. You may not be big enough to be a leader in the market, but you surely can protect yourself and take positive steps to improve turnover in general, and with high-margin products in particular.

The Computer and the Small Company

When your company has reached the stage where a computer seems appropriate, certain precautions are important. First, identify the *primary* reason you are considering a computer, and have that application drive your purchase. For example, if your primary motivation is to control an inventory with 2,000 separate items, you want plenty of memory and some solid inventory software, not some fancy package to do your financial statements. A sub-contractor should concentrate on getting a first-rate job costing package, tailored to that particular trade if possible. A good estimating package would probably be helpful to a sub-contractor, as it would be to an engineering firm. For the latter, engineering graphics capability might be the most important of all.

Once you have identified your primary need and the hardware/software combination which can best serve that need, then *and only then,* should you even consider other applications. In fact, if there is little computer sophistication or experience in your company, you may want to delay any other applications (even the so-called standard ones) until your staff has adjusted to having a computer on the premises and has learned to run it (not the other way around) on a straight-forward, one-step-at-a-time basis. If you are going to make a computer startup error, make it by going too slowly, not too fast. You can always catch up, but you can seldom fully recover your losses from a computer disaster.

One final piece of advice in this regard: Whatever application you are starting should be run as before on your old reliable manual system at the same time (in parallel) for three months or until you are getting the same results from both systems, whichever comes later. Forget what the computer salesman says on this subject. See the identical results with your own eyes before even considering discontinuing your manual system.

5

BANK RELATIONS

- ❏ Introduction
- ❏ Choosing a Loan Officer
- ❏ Applying For a Loan
- ❏ Company Financial Status
- ❏ Ability to Repay
- ❏ Use of Loan Funds
- ❏ The Quality of Management
- ❏ Terms and Conditions
- ❏ Personal Guarantee
- ❏ Miscellany

BANK RELATIONS

Introduction

Typically, the small businessman views bankers solely as a source of:

1. Venture capital

2. Debt financing

3. Equipment loans

4. Working capital

5. Accounts receivable financing

6. Short-term debt

7. Long-term debt

While the underlying purpose of a bank is some kind of debt financing, there is much more to this relationship than simply the granting of a loan. The small company manager has every right to expect at least the following from a good banker:

1. Appropriately risked debt financing.

2. Assistance in foreseeing and/or recognizing problems, and in distinguishing management problems from purely financial difficulties.

3. Appropriate referrals to other competent professionals.

4. Understanding, patience and realistic friendship.

You've probably heard the old saw about bankers lending money only when you don't need it. While there is some truth in this aphorism, the fact remains that bankers are in the business of lending money, and your company is a potential customer. Keep in mind that banks compete with one another, and they are competing for *your* business. Feel free to shop around for the best relationship and the best deal.

Choosing a Loan Officer

The single most crucial quality to look for in a loan officer is that he or she knows something about business and not just about banking. You need an individual who will truly understand the fundamental differences among various kinds of businesses, as well as the more subtle differences among individual companies within an industry group. Particularly important is the ability to grasp what it's like to run a small company — the sudden turns of events, the periodic cash binds, the very real risks and the very real opportunities. Verify this capacity through the loan officer's personal customer portfolio and knowledgeability about your type of business.

Choose a loan officer with adequate lending authority to handle your company's present needs and provide considerable room for growth. Therefore, you should try hard not to entrust your borrowing capacity, or the integrity of an outstanding loan, to an individual who has to clear all decisions with superiors and/or a loan committee. You cannot tell how much your presentation will lose in translation.

Make sure that the loan officer you choose earns your respect and confidence in the first interview. First impressions tend to be accurate in banking relations. Your loan officer should give clear evidence that he or she will receive bad news in a thoughtful and mature manner — not just push the panic button. An impulsive move by a panicky loan officer at just the wrong time could jeopardize the very existence of your company.

Some of the smaller banks will attempt to be more creative and aggressive in their pursuit of your business than the larger ones. Also, you can switch your account with relative ease to a larger bank when the time comes, as long as your company is successful. But the bank in question should be large enough to grow with your company for at least two years, and to provide all the business services (e.g. international) you may need. If you plan to do business with a large bank at any location other than the headquarter's office, deal with one of that bank's major commercial (business loan) branches.

Finally, evaluate the quality of the loan package drawn up for your company. Most importantly, note the degree to which it meets your current needs, anticipates future needs and correctly assesses your ability to repay pursuant to specific loan terms and conditions.

Referrals from business acquaintances and professionals should provide the names of at least a half dozen loan officers and banks fitting the above profile. Interview at least three. If your loan officer will supply the names of a few customers of similar size and business status, so much the better.

Ideally, you should choose your bank and loan officer at least one full year before you ask for funds. During the pre-loan-request period, keep your loan officer fully informed of your company's progress. A quarterly lunch and presentation of financial statements should be the minimum of informative contact. Include the bad news along with the good. Get your loan officer used to your problems, as well as your brilliant successes. It will give him or her a greater feeling of confidence that you can weather storms and surprises, a feeling which will be to your benefit when you ask for money and throughout the term of the loan.

A word of advice: If you do establish a relationship with a large bank far in advance of your need for funds, be prepared for the sudden departure of your hand-picked loan officer. This phenomenon is particularly prevalent in the branches. Therefore, be sure to get to know the other loan officers in the branch, and insist that one other specific officer has been assigned to your account and is familiar with it.

Applying For a Loan

Assuming that you have cultivated a banking relationship well in advance of your need for funds, your loan officer should be reasonably familiar with your company's overall financial condition and recent performance; however, an update will be in order. The loan officer will be looking at four elements with utmost care:

1. Your company's current financial status (both short- and long-term) as indicated by the balance sheet;

2. Your company's ability to repay, as indicated by your most recent income statement and your projections of future profits and cash flow;

3. The reasonableness of the business use of the loan proceeds, both in terms of the likely return on investment and the match between short- or long-term term financing and short- or long-term needs;

4. Perhaps most important of all, the quality of management.

Company Financial Status

When preparing your loan request, pay particular attention to your company's financial status, as discussed in Chapters 3 and 4. Key ratios and gross and net profit margins will be critical. Do not spare any effort in developing a clear written/oral presentation, and ensure that you have adequate answers to all logical questions.

Ability to Repay

A loan officer will not loan money to any individual or company without a definable source of repayment. Even loans collateralized by tangible assets (such as equipment) must pass the test of ability to repay. Collateral will frequently cover only a portion of a bank's loss, and it is management's utilization of the collateral, and not the collateral itself, which provides the income from which debt service cash is generated.

The surest indicator of ability to repay is the Income Statement, also referred to as the Profit and Loss Statement or P&L. In the absence of a major event (not the loan itself) which effectively changes the very kind of company you have, a history of P&L's going back at least three years will be among the most important financial information you will submit with your loan application.

Pre-tax profit ("Bottom Line") will receive immediate and lasting consideration. If you are able to achieve profits of at least 10 percent of Net Sales, you will likely impress your loan officer. If your profit margin is much less than 10 percent, or if your company is unprofitable, you had better be prepared with sensible explanations as to why your past results are not relevant for predicting future performance.

In many ways, the components of the P&L areas are as important as the bottom line. Not infrequently, for example, a small company will live in virtual squalor in the beginning to preserve meager resources, and, if successful, will achieve a relatively high level of pre-tax profitability by keeping overhead to a bare minimum. While this is commendable and indicative of conservative management, many bankers will be aware that overhead cannot be held down artificially forever, and will make allowance for such future increases.

With the historical profit performance firmly in mind, your loan officer will probably turn full attention to your projections of future profits and cash flow. These projections represent your most tangible statement as to your ability to repay the loan. They must, above all, be realistic. If your projections significantly exceed historical performance (without adequate justification) they will hinder your loan application by damaging your credibility.

Since projections represent a view of the future, they are necessarily based on assumptions. It is these assumptions which must be able to withstand close scrutiny. What makes you say that your sales are going to increase by 30 percent per year for five years? On what grounds do you claim that your gross profit will increase from its historical level of 35 percent to 50 percent in just 12 months? How can you possibly expect to double your sales without increasing your overhead? If your answers to questions like these are vague or incredible, you'll probably have to find another bank.

As discussed previously, cash flow projections are derived largely from projections of profit and loss, but reflect *only* the checkbook. Therefore, non-cash expenses like depreciation are out and expenditures for, say, capital equipment are recorded as "cash disbursed," despite their amortization for tax and P&L purposes. In addition, it is critically important to add a contingency in your cash flow projection. There is nothing worse than having to go back to your banker after a relatively short time to report that your loan has proven to be insufficient to cover your needs.

Use of Loan Funds

Your loan officer will look at the use of the funds for which you are applying from at least two standpoints: first, the likely return on investment and, second, the matchup between the kind of loan you are requesting and the use to which you are putting it. The key question in all this is: What will the company be able to do with this money which it could not do without it, and, as a result, what new profits will it generate? Once again we are talking about the reasonableness of your assumptions and the credibility of your figures.

If you are requesting a working capital credit line, without which your company's growth will be sorely restricted, then your return on investment will come from the profits earned on the additional sales. Investment in capital equipment or plant can pay off in a similar manner, or by allowing you to reduce your cost of goods sold (and increase your gross profit.) How you go about calculating return on investment is far less important than the reasonableness of the assumptions underlying your calculation. Anything from a simple payback method to sophisticated discounted cash flows is acceptable. If anything, be wary of over-sophistication at the small company level.

The extent to which your loan request properly matches the type of loan with the use of funds will demonstrate to your loan officer how much you understand the fundamentals of financial management. The prevailing rule is to use short-term financing (an annually reviewed accounts receivable line, for example) for short-term needs (working capital.) Long-term financing (a term loan for a fixed number of years) is for long-term needs (say, equipment or property purchases.) The logic behind this rule goes back to the ability to repay.

For example, if a company has favorable current and quick ratios, but lacks cash because so much money is tied up in the receivables generated from rapidly increasing sales, a receivables line can ease the cash situation and relieve management from making expedient short-term financial decisions which may not be in the company's long-term interest. But, importantly, the money is there in the current assets in the form of receivables which can reasonably be expected to turn into cash within 90 days. (By the way, be aware in this regard that bankers don't like old accounts receivable any better than you do, and will often stipulate that receivables over 90 days are removed as collateral against which you can draw on your line of credit.)

By the same token, favorable ratios of debt coverage* and equity to long-term debt will assist

---

*Debt Coverage Ratio $= \dfrac{\text{Profit Before Interest and Taxes}}{\text{Debt Service (Principal and Interest)}}$

you to get the term loan, whether you collateralize it or not. This condition indicates that there are values in the balance sheet which could be applied to paying back the loan. Also, it shows that either: 1) the stockholders are taking a considerable risk in the form of capital contributions, or 2) management has generated considerable Retained Earnings. Either or both of these situations are close to the top of your loan officer's list of desirable features in any loan application.

The Quality of Management

The quality of management is probably the most important, though the least tangible, of all factors influencing whether you will get your loan, and under what terms and conditions. All the figures in the world are useless if the top management group as a whole, and especially the president, are not equal to the task ahead. How a banker makes that determination is dependent upon his or her temperament and the extent to which you have a confidence-building track record. The loan officer will be looking for tangible historical results and credible projections.

Terms and Conditions

Finally a word about the makeup of the bank's loan proposal. "Terms" refers to the loan itself, and includes such items as:

1. Loan Amount

2. Interest Rate (fixed or floating with the prime rate)

3. Availability/Expiration (the period during which the company may tap the available funds)

4. Maturity (the date at which any term loan taken out by the company during the availability period matures and is due for repayment)

5. Whether secured or unsecured. Obviously unsecured is better. If secured, see #6 below.

6. Collateral (the bank's security.) Try to keep all collateral pegged to specific loans, e.g. Accounts Receivable.* A general "filing" or security agreement on all your company's assets filed with the state is a matter of public record and to be avoided, if possible.

7. Compensating Balances (required deposits to be kept with the bank.) While the typical reaction to this request is, "Why borrow your own money?", it is a fact that comp. balances will reduce the loan interest rate. So it isn't simply a one-sided deal in the bank's favor.

"Conditions" refers first to acceptable balance sheet factors which the company must maintain to keep the loan available. There are typically required minima in your:

1. Ratio of total debt to equity

2. Ratio of cash flow to funded debt (principal payments)

*A loan against inventory will frequently be part of a receivables loan package, because of the cycle of inventory to receivables to cash, thence reinvested in new inventory.

3. Current ratio

4. Working capital

5. Net worth

6. Debt coverage ratio

Some banks will also ask for goals to be met in these areas by a specified date. Debt coverage is of particular concern to the bank loan officer, since it bears directly on the customer's ability to repay. A ratio of 1.25:1 to 2:1 reflects a generally acceptable range.

Second are management actions which are typically required (1 and 2 below) or prohibited without written bank approval (3, 4 and 5.)

1. Providing income statements and balance sheets on a timely basis

2. Providing other documentation to the bank as necessary

3. Borrowings outside the normal course of business

4. Dividends or repurchase of outstanding stock

5. Mergers or acquisitions

A typical loan agreement commitment letter from a major bank is presented in Exhibit 11.

Personal Guarantee

It is easy to see that the sum total of these various terms and conditions is to protect the bank's interest by keeping management from going off the

Exhibit 11

Sample Commitment Letter
Line of Credit

January 2, 1984

It is my pleasure to inform you that _____ (Bank) is prepared to offer _____ the following line of credit. The terms and conditions required by the Bank for the continuation of this line are as follows:

Amount: $250,000 revolving line of credit with facility for a maximum of $100,000 in letters of credit.

Rate: Prime plus two percent (P + 2.00%) floating, interest payable monthly. Interest to be figured on a 360 day year.

Advances: Advances to be made in accordance with each non-negotiable Order to Pay Loan Funds executed by Borrower and received by Bank.

Maturity: January 2, 1985

Collateral: Security Agreement covering all inventories and accounts receivable.

121

Exhibit 11 (continued)

Other Terms and Conditions

1. Borrower to provide Bank with a Corporate Resolution to Borrow in the amount of $250,000.

2. Borrower to provide Bank with monthly company prepared financial statements to include Balance Sheet and Income Statement no later than 30 days following month-end. Annual CPA compiled statements to be forwarded to the Bank no later than 60 days after fiscal year-end.

3. Borrower to provide Bank with a perfected first interest in all Accounts Receivable and inventory.

4. Borrower to provide Bank with monthly Accounts Receivable agings no later than 15 days after month-end.

5. Borrower to have minimum Working Capital of $250,000 and a minimum Current Ratio of 1.5:1.

6. Borrower to have a minimum Tangible Net Worth of $400,000 and a maximum Debt divided by Tangible Net Worth of 1.5:1.

7. Borrower to maintain net free collected demand deposits* in an amount no less than 10% of the committment ($25,000).

*Compensating balances

Exhibit 11 (continued)

Borrower shall pay a fee equal to Prime plus two and one-half percent (P + 2.5%) on the shortfall monthly beginning April 20, 1984.

If the terms and conditions of this line are acceptable with you, please acknowledge by signing the copy of this letter before January 10, 1984 at which time this committment expires.

Sincerely,

Financial Services Officer

deep end with the bank's money. There is one more condition which probably does more in this regard than all the others combined: the personal guarantee.

Except on rare occasions, a bank loan for a small company is usually guaranteed personally by the owner (and spouse.) If your company has enough leverage with the bank, then you will not have to sign a personal guarantee; if not, you will. The amount of leverage you have with the bank is strictly a matter of who needs whom more; so don't expend an unnecessary amount of energy on this point. The main thing is to get the loan package drawn up to meet your company's needs as to type of loan(s), interest rate, terms and conditions. As long as you have confidence in the future of your company, the only practical influence of your personal guarantee is that you have to list it under Contingent Liabilities on your personal balance sheet. Since it is very likely that any personal borrowing would be from the same bank, the significance of that is very limited.

Miscellany

Be prepared to ask your bank to write a side letter to the detailed proposal which spells out (without the terms and conditions) the size and time frames of your available bank debt. Such a letter can come in very handy in dealing with bonding companies, for example. If you can use such a document to advantage, don't be shy about asking for it.

Finally, don't let the fact that you have put a great deal of time and effort into a potential banking relationship dissuade you from pitching the whole thing overboard if you are convinced that you can do substantially better elsewhere. While it would be clearly preferable to make that determination before you receive the bank's formal proposal, remember that a poor decision can have far-reaching implications. You don't want to pull out at the last minute without good and substantial reasons, especially when money is tight. But if you have sufficient justification, follow your best judgment regardless of the stage of your negotiations.

6

CREDIT AND COLLECTION

- ❑ Introduction
- ❑ Tough Credit Policies
- ❑ Evaluating Credit References
- ❑ Other Credit Considerations
- ❑ Maximizing Usable Accounting
      Information
- ❑ Improving Collection Procedures
- ❑ Cash Discounts

CREDIT AND COLLECTION

Introduction

Ask 100 small company presidents what they see as the most serious threat to small companies during a recession, and probably 95 will respond, "Lost sales." Serious as lost sales can be, however, management can often compensate by scaling down inventories, payroll, and other expenses. But if companies maintain healthy sales levels (and the cash outlays necessary to support those sales) and cannot collect their receivables, the companies' very survival can be jeopardized. At the least, high interest rates and slow collections can sorely strain the financial resources of most small businesses. This chapter presents some practical, tested methods for improving collection procedures.

Tough Credit Policies

The best way to avoid collection problems is to avoid giving credit to potential deadbeats in the first place. While it is axiomatic that no sale, however large, is worth making if you cannot collect, most salespersons instinctively side with potential customers in credit matters. Therefore, management must retain responsibility for granting credit. Credit policy making should never be ceded to the sales force, because the risks are simply too great. What, then, should credit policies be?

First, make clear to all concerned that only the president can overrule the credit manager or accounting supervisor on credit matters. Some time ago, a computer hardware manufacturer I know shipped $20,000 worth of merchandise to a new customer at the directions of the marketing vice president, despite the strenuous objections of the credit manager. The company is still trying to collect on that account.

Second, and perhaps obviously, never make delivery of goods or services on credit until credit for the amount of the proposed sale has actually been cleared. Exercise similar caution in ordering or manufacturing inventory which would not have a ready market with other customers. When companies get in financial trouble, they often look for second sources to supplement suppliers which may be lost because of slow payment.

Any time you grant credit to an unknown, even on one initial order, you are taking unnecessary risks with your receivables. A percentage of these new accounts is bound to turn sour and, during an economic downturn, that percentage will increase dramatically. Any and all deliveries prior to credit clearance should be made on a C.O.D. basis. Your salespeople may not like it, but they will not like a subsequent chargeback against commission either or, worse, poor company cash flow jeopardizing their jobs.

Third, obtain an adequate number of credit references, and check them thoroughly. While ratings can be helpful, they cannot replace first-hand credit information. There should be a minimum of three trade references, preferably local so they can be telephoned inexpensively.

Bank references can also be helpful, but they should not be used as substitutes for trade references. Many bankers are reluctant to provide the most helpful kind of financial information. This potential customer of yours is already a customer of the bank, so even a most scrupulous banker may use some rose coloring when portraying the condition of a borrower.

Evaluating Credit References

When checking trade references, seek to answer the following questions: How long has the company been a customer? What has been the high credit? Is there currently a credit limit? What has been the payment record, especially during the past six months? Does this company typically pay within terms? Does it pick up discounts with any frequency? Has the pattern of any of these behaviors changed significantly during the past six months? Finally, can the management be trusted to keep its promises? Most companies experience financial difficulty at some time, but if management can be trusted, you will probably be paid eventually. NOTE: Your banker may be able to make some productive, discreet inquiries for certain prospective customers, especially local ones.

If you use a trade reference checking service, be sure to spot-check the results. One company I worked with lost $2,000 because the customer set up phony references which had passed the checking service.

Few prospective customers would knowingly give out bad credit references. So anything less than a good reference should be considered a bad reference. Never settle for surface gloss. Probe for hidden weaknesses, such as a contractor without a state license, and pursue any negative indication. If you have any doubts, however slight, you may want to impose a credit limit. Thus, even if your initial judgment is faulty or if your customer's financial condition suddenly deteriorates, you will limit your risk.

Other Credit Considerations

While some argue for extending liberal credit terms to maximize market penetration at the expense of more financially strapped or conservative competitors, I contend that this argument is fundamentally weak. For one thing, high costs associated with carrying receivables would require you either to raise prices or to lose profits. Worse, you inevitably attract an increasing percentage of new customers who could not deal with you were it not for the extra 30 or 60 days you are granting. The financial instability and insecurity inherent in such customer relations should be avoided, not encouraged.

Finally, do not be influenced by friendship when your judgment tells you a company is in financial trouble. A number of years ago, the head of a client company was reticent, for strictly personal reasons, to pressure a long overdue customer by holding up the Christmas order until the account was cleared. When the customer went bankrupt a few months later, my client's thank you was ten cents on the dollar.

Maximizing Usable Accounting Information

Your accounts receivable collection effort will be no better than the accuracy and timeliness of your accounting information. Whether you use ledger cards, a computer, or something else, information on shipments and payments must be posted as quickly as possible. How else, for example, can you be sure a customer has not exceeded the credit limit? The most useful summary display of this information is the accounts receivable aging, normally pulled from accounting source records at the end of each month. (See Exhibit 12.)

This format seems quite straightforward. "Current" denotes the month just ended, "30 days" denotes the previous month, and so on. There is not much room for improvement here, or so it would seem. Actually, every heading between "Current" and "Prior" is terribly misleading. The reality is that all receivables in the 30 day column are *over* 30 days old. Assuming that the deliveries reflected in that column were made evenly over the course of the month, the average age of the receivables in the

Exhibit 12

Typical Format For
Accounts Receivable Aging

Customer	Current	30 Days	60 Days	90 Days	Prior	Total
A						
B						
C						
Total						

30-day column is 45 days, a significant difference. Succeeding columns indicate an age of 75 and 105 days respectively.

To turn this reporting problem into an opportunity, I recommend a simple format revision, dividing the Current column into the first and second halves of the month just concluded. Thus the first column of the January 31 aging would be headed "January 1-15" and the second column, "January 16-31." This provides two distinct advantages:

First, it allows you to get at least a half-month head start in running down overdues. For example, if your terms are net 30 days, you know positively that every receivable in the second column (first half of the month) is past due on the 16th of the month following delivery, since, by definition, all second-column receivables reflect deliveries made on the 15th of the previous month or earlier. Therefore, you can start your follow-up procedure then, instead of waiting for the February 28 aging to be completed two or three weeks later. You can use that extra time to uncover problems of non-delivery, partial shipment, damaged merchandise, customer dissatisfaction, or any of the myriad of problems which make collections so much more difficult after 90 or 120 days.

The best way to keep a receivable out of the 90-day column is to keep it out of the 60-day column; and the best way to prevent that is to keep it out of the 30-day column. This format, along with aggressive collection efforts during these extra two or three weeks, can help you achieve that objective.

Second, this format allows you to calculate more accurately the average age of your receivables, which aids in comparing your accounts receivable status from one month to the next. The most common method for calculating average age is simply to divide total sales for the most recent fiscal year, or the most recent 12-month period, by the number of days in the year to get the average sales per day. Then divide total receivables by the result of the previous calculation to get the age of receivables in days.

The flaw in this method is that it makes no provision for the spread of the receivables among the various aging columns. Thus, $200,000 in the 90-day column would have exactly the same average age as $200,000 in the Current column. Little help for management can be gleaned from such a superficial analysis. Compare the weighted average calculation shown in Exhibit 13 for the period ending January 31, 1981.

By multiplying the total receivable dollars in the first column by the average age of that column (7.5 days) we get $300,000 days. We then perform this same calculation in each of the remaining columns, with a judgment factor for the average age in the Prior column. Next, the sum of the dollar-days column totals is divided by total receivables. The resulting weighted average is a far more accurate figure for the average age of the receivables, and one which is more readily comparable from month to month and year to year.

If your company is a general contractor or subcontractor, you are probably well aware of the

Exhibit 13

Recommended Format For Accounts Receivable Aging
January 31, 1981 (in thousands)

Customer	Jan. 16-31	Jan. 1-15	Dec.	Nov.	Oct.	Prior	Total
A	$ 10	$ 5					$ 15
B	15	10					25
C	8	15					23
D	7	10					17
E			$ 20	$ 10	$ 10		40
Total	$ 40	$ 40	$ 20	$ 10	$ 10	$0	$120
	x7.5 days	x22.5	x45	x75	x105		
	$ 300 days	$900	$900	$750	$1,050		

```
$  300 days
    900
    900
    750
  1,050
$3,900 days ÷ $120 = 32.5 days
```

137

impact of retentions on your overall collection status. (Retentions are the portion of the bill, often 10%, held back by the customer until all your work is deemed satisfactory.) Take, for example, the relative average age of receivables of a contractor client, with retentions both omitted and included. (See Exhibit 14.) Note that many more dollar-days are involved in retentions than in all other receivables combined. Also, retentions have increased the average age of receivables by more than a month, while tying up nearly $100,000 in cash.

In addition to being particularly aggressive in collecting retentions (and all other receivables if you have much money tied up in retentions), you should control your percentage of new construction jobs, since these are where retentions tend to be most common and severe.

Improving Collection Procedures

When formulating your collection policies and procedures, remember that firmness and consistency are far more important than fairness. Let your competitors settle for an average age of 50 to 75 days. You should strive for 30 days and should settle for no more than 45 days. All it takes is an early start and dogged determination.

As receivables get older, you must get progressively tougher. The matrix in Exhibit 15 suggests a series of progressive measures you can employ. The essential element is consistent implementation of your collection policies. Once a receivable is past due according to your published terms,

Exhibit 14

Average Age of Receivables With and Without Retentions

Without Retentions:

	Current	30-59 days	60-89 days	90-119 days	120 + days
	$ 441,434	$118,912	$1,610	$9,712	$95,064
	× 15	× 45	× 75	× 105	× 150
	$ 6,621,510 days	$5,351,040	$120,750	$1,019,760	$14,259,600

$ 6,621,510 days
5,351,040
120,750
1,019,760
14,259,600

$27,372,660 days ÷ $666,732 (total accounts receivable without retentions) = **41 days**

Exhibit 14 (continued)

With Retentions:

Average age of retentions = 180 days (conservative estimate)

Retentions: $199,984
            × 180 days

$ 35,997,120 days
+ 27,372,660 days (total dollar-days without retentions)
$ 63,369,780 days ÷ $866,715 (total accounts receivable)

= **73 days**

Exhibit 15

Suggested Collection Procedures According to Age of Accounts Receivable

	30 Days	45 Days	60 Days	75 Days	90 Days
Communication	Telephone & Letter	Telephone & Letter	Telephone & Letter	Telephone & Letter	Letter
Message	Overdue. Please Pay.	Pay in 15 days or will stop shipments.	Have stopped shipments. Pay now.	Pay in 15 days or will turn over to collection, small claims court, etc.	Am taking action previously cited.
Action	None	None	Stop shipments.	None	Take action previously cited.

141

you have more right to the money than your customer does.

Be aggressive in your collection effort. Establish as personal a relationship as possible with those responsible for paying the bills. Among small company customers, those responsible will usually be the president, controller, or bookkeeper; thus, they are easy to identify and locate. In larger companies, the accounts payable department processes payables, so it is important to find out specifically how bills are paid and by whom. Not infrequently, for example, payables in large companies are divided among payables clerks alphabetically by supplier. But these procedures and responsibilities vary from one company to another, so you should become acquainted with each system and use it to your advantage.

Get to know the individuals who can influence how quickly you will be paid. Let them know that yours is a small company and that quick turnover of money is critical for your success. You would be surprised how favorably many large company employees react.

When attempting to collect an overdue receivable, exact a specific and personal promise for payment. Write down the promise and who made it on a key receivable sheet. Not only will this procedure allow you to keep track of collections more easily, it will give you a greater feeling of confidence and controlled righteous indignation when following up on broken promises.

Don't believe anyone in an accounts payable department who tells you that payments are computer controlled and that the process cannot be interrupted or circumvented. Any company, large or small, has the capability to handwrite checks.

Cash Discounts

In some industries, cash discounts are so deeply rooted that all suppliers must use them. If the practice does not prevail in your industry, the factors to consider in determining whether to offer cash discounts to your customers are similar to those for deciding whether to pick up supplier discounts. First, consider the availability of cash. If you are frequently in a cash bind and additional debt to alleviate the situation is not readily available, then cash discounts could improve cash flow.

Next, consider the cost, i.e. the effective discount interest rate. The most common discount interest calculation shows, for example, that a cash discount of 2% to pay 30 days sooner (say, in 10 days rather than 40) reflects an annual interest rate of 24% (2% for 1 month times 12 months). Not so obvious is the fact that a large proportion of customers picking up this new cash discount may already be paying within terms. So, in effect, you may be paying much more than the 24% annual interest just cited to get your slow payers speeded up.

Thus, before starting something which may be difficult to stop, analyze carefully your mix of receivables to determine whether cash discounts will solve more problems than they create. As a rule, try to keep your effective discount interest rate no more than one percentage point higher than the rate at which you borrow, unless you are strapped for cash.

7

Outside Professionals

- ❑ C.P.A.
- ❑ Attorney
- ❑ Management Consultant
- ❑ What to Look For
- ❑ Checking References
- ❑ The Interview
- ❑ Getting Results

OUTSIDE PROFESSIONALS

C.P.A.

When seeking the services of an outside
C.P.A., first and foremost you must determine your
needs and internal capabilities. The type and amount
of outside accounting assistance appropriate for
your company will depend to a large degree on
whether your company does or does not have any
of the following:

Public stockholders: This will require that you
retain a well known firm, which will perform a
certified (expensive) audit. Given the level of
regulation of publicly traded shares, there is no
choice on this matter.

Volume sufficient to justify a full-charge inside
bookkeeper: As stated previously, this is the
preferred method of accounting for small companies for reasons of timeliness and the acces-
sibility to backup data. If you can find and
afford a qualified full-charge bookkeeper, hire
one.

A business common and uncomplicated enough to allow efficient utilization of its inside or outside computer: Much of accounting is routine, and your business may be one which can utilize "canned" software already available. But if, for any reason, you must customize your software substantially, or if you currently have an accounting staff which is unfamiliar with, and afraid of, computers, you would be well advised to stay with your manual system until at least one of these conditions changes.

An extraordinary need for tax advice: Such can be provided either by a highly qualified tax C.P.A. or by a tax attorney.

Sufficient cash flow to allow management to choose the best the profession has to offer.

There are literally hundreds of C.P.A.'s in each major geographical area, divided into three categories; first, the "Big-8" firms which are generally too expensive; second, one- or two-person shops, which are generally overloaded and make most of their profits from providing tax advice, rather than genuinely useful small company monthly statements; third, a relatively few small-to-medium-size firms (say six to eighteen professionals) which can really do the job for you. Find a firm of this type, and you will have made a major step in the improvement of your financial information. Written expectations from both sides would be a useful exercise.

Referrals, especially from bankers, can be

quite helpful in your search. Be sure to interview at least three or four prospective C.P.A.'s, with particular reference to general competence, fee schedules, accuracy of estimated costs, ease of personal relationship and potential growth. Ensure a high level of competence and experience in your particular industry. Related experience in other industries is not good enough. There are simply too many other C.P.A.'s to choose from to settle for anything less, and the ethical standards of the profession are high enough that you should not have to be concerned about the confidentiality of your financial information.

Attorney

There are only two categories of tasks which your attorney should be allowed to perform for you and your company:

1. Provide competent and timely legal advice on matters within his or her particular area(s) of legal expertise.

2. Draft all necessary legal documentation pursuant to your specific instructions as to purpose and direction.

Areas into which only a most extraordinary attorney should be permitted to intrude are:

1. Advice on how to run your company.

2. Direct negotiations with anyone, at least until the substance of an agreement has been reached between you and the other party.

No more than one attorney in 100 has any significant knowledge about running a small company. The fastest way I know to foul up a deal is to get a lawyer involved too soon. Clearly, the function of the attorney is to ensure that you have considered all possible pitfalls in advance, and make adequate provision for them. The most effective way to do that is to develop a business program which appears to meet your requirements, and then discuss it with your attorney. In the case of a major deal with an outside party, develop jointly the structure of that deal, reduce it to a non-legally-binding memorandum of understanding and, only then, go to your attorney for the drafting of definitive legal documents.

Referrals, especially from bankers, will again be helpful in your search for a qualified attorney. Interviewing at least three or four attorneys and reference checking as with the C.P.A. will be essential. For most companies, one good corporate attorney is sufficient. You must determine, first of all, if your company is like most others in this respect. If not, identify specific areas of competence which you require, (patent or maritime, for example) and search out attorneys in each, as you would medical specialists. Don't wait until you need an attorney to find one.

Management Consultant

From the perspective of a small company management consultant, one of the most appealing views of that professional's role is that of "business doctor." This concept conjures up images of the corporate patient lying prostrate on the floor with its vital signs barely perceptible. The consultant makes an office call, ministers to the patient from a black bag of perfect solutions and quickly returns the patient to robust health. Unfortunately, this picture bears little resemblance to reality. In fact, articles in leading business journals over the years, such as "Consultants – Cure or Cancer in the Corporate Body" and "Consultants – Who Needs Them?", remind all of us in the profession that outside consulting advice is often imperfect or, worse, counterproductive.

Most importantly, a small company management consultant is a vehicle for change. This change can be promoted through four primary avenues:

1. The mere presence of the consultant stimulating thought and action by management and, not infrequently, an increase in productivity by the workforce.

2. Dialogue and searching questions – not necessarily brilliant questions, just the right ones for the particular company and situation.

3. Specific recommendations, preferably formulated in concert with management, and reflecting a consensus.

4. Assistance with implementation – important in small companies, in which managers wear many hats, work long hours and have difficulty supervising major projects in addition to running day-to-day business activities.

Not infrequently, the consultant will be called in to assist in finding a solution to a problem which actually reflects a symptom, rather than a fundamental disease. It is of the utmost importance that the consultant ensure that the *real* problem(s) be addressed in a meaningful way in an atmosphere of calm and confidence, especially in serious trouble situations.

The consultant must further ensure that areas of action are limited to those which management can understand and relate to, and in doses which management can absorb. Every small company management team has significant strengths and weaknesses. The role of any outside advisor is to assist that management to develop programs which will work in that particular environment. There is no special art or skill in coming up with solutions to small company problems which should work in theory. Any intelligent recent business school graduate is more than qualified to perform that task. Rather, the effective consultant is distinguished by his or her ability to choose from among the array of possible approaches those which are particularly appropriate to the management team which will implement them.

Small company managers are often resistant to the idea of bringing in an outside business advisor. Many of the fears behind this resistance have considerable validity, principal among which is a fear of excessive cost. Fees are openly discussed ahead of time, verbally and/or in writing, but frequently balloon as the project proceeds. The manager thus finds himself in the position of sacrificing consulting costs already sunk or accepting a total bill much higher than budget. There is also a fear of lost valuable time through involvement in hiring and working with a consultant or firm.

Often there is justifiable dismay in the "selling job" by the prospective consultant, exhibiting a lack of any semblance of modesty ("We can do anything.") or consideration for the feelings of the client. ("Anything you can do we can do better.") Somebody "sells" the service but somebody else will actually do the work. (When I say "we", I really mean "they".) This kind of approach will frequently reinforce the manager's natural reluctance to appear to admit failure to the consultant, to subordinates or even to himself. As well, it can appear to lend credence to an often unstated fear of information leaks to competitors. While this last fear is usually unjustified, the manager will tend to focus more on the penalty than the probability.

What to Look For

Most important in a prospective management consultant is an impressive ability to grasp essential problems, as well as a demonstrable "fit" between the consulting capabilities needed and the skills and/or background of the prospective consultant. You should be convinced that this individual or firm is clearly distinguished from the competition. Perhaps this differentiation will be in the form of a particular area of expertise, or knowledge of an important market segment. Perhaps it will be nothing more than a perceptible superiority over his competitors. The prospective consultant should be willing to admit the limits of his or her ability and those of the firm. There is no substitute for the truth, and puffery should be summarily dismissed along with its source. Finally, the consultant should present effective and relevant references.

You must feel free to give out as much confidential information as the consultant is likely to need to make a determination as to his capability to perform the assignment, as well as estimate fees. If a non-disclosure agreement is appropriate (see Exhibit 16 for sample) then secure one. Be certain that the one who presents the proposal in person is the one who will actually do the work. Analyze carefully the quality of the questions put forward in this interview. Make certain that this professional knows how to probe, understands the "detective work" aspects of consulting. If this individual does not satisfactorily display these qualities in an opening interview, prospects are dim that they will become more evident as the relationship grows.

Finally, ensure that the prospective consultant has demonstrated a willingness to "roll up his sleeves" and work with management in all phases of the project, especially in the implementation of recommendations. All too many consultants place too much emphasis on thick reports which tend to be read late, misunderstood and implemented poorly if at all. The consultant who breezes in, analyzes the situation, writes a report and leaves has typically performed an expensive disservice for the small company.

Exhibit 16

Sample Non-Disclosure Agreement

(Name of individual and/or company releasing information) hereinafter referred to as "Discloser" and (name of individual and/or company receiving information) hereinafter referred to as "Recipient" have concluded that it is in the interest of both parties that Discloser provide Recipient with certain proprietary and confidential information. This agreement sets forth the conditions under which such information is to be provided to Recipient.

1. The proprietary information concerns the following:

2. This information may be in the form of, but not necessarily limited to, the following: plans, designs, drawings, specifications, prototypes, customer lists, market data, ideas.

3. Recipient shall exercise all reasonable precautions to prevent disclosure of such information to any third party, except as expressly authorized in writing by Discloser.

4. Internal distribution of such information to employees of Recipient shall be strictly limited to personnel with a clear and specific need to know, and shall occur only after any and all such employees have signed a copy of this agreement.

5. The purpose for which Recipient and/or employees of Recipient shall use this information is as follows:

Exhibit 16 (continued)

6. Use of this information for any other purpose, except as subsequently authorized in writing by Discloser, is strictly prohibited.

7. This agreement shall be construed and governed in accordance with the laws of the state of _____ .

Should any clause be unenforceable, the remainder of this agreement shall remain in full force and effect.

Discloser:

_____
(Name)
(Company)

Recipient:

_____
(Name)
(Company)

Checking References

When checking the references of a prospective consultant, or any other professional for that matter, certain questions are of particular relevance.

1. *Exactly* what was the task?

2. How well was it performed?

3. Were his recommendations implemented?

4. With his help?

5. How well did he work with top management and others in the company?

6. Did you receive adequate value for the money you spent?

7. Given similar problems and/or circumstances, WOULD YOU HIRE HIM AGAIN?

The Interview

Obviously, the interview will play an important role in your selection of a consultant. In this regard, remember that the personal relationship you develop with this professional will have a significant impact on his effectiveness. A warm rapport is much more conducive to a relaxed, sober consideration of facts and options than a cold, sterile atmosphere. While credentials are important, they aren't everything. So if you don't like a particular professional, for whatever reason, look elsewhere. It will be worth the additional time and effort. There are enough consultants, even in the narrowest professional context, to enable you to avoid starting a relationship which is less than promising.

Getting Results

Central to working effectively with your consultant is a clear definition of the scope of the work. This definition will depend chiefly on three factors:

1. How self-contained the project is.

2. How much trouble there is within the company.

3. How certain consultant and client are that the real problems have been identified.

The broader the assignment, the more trouble in the company, the less certain the diagnosis, then the wider the scope of work and the fewer the restrictions on the consultant's activities. A solid plan of approach, arrived at jointly by consultant and client, is essential. If this plan is clearly understood by all, a brief outline should be more than adequate. There should be reasonable flexibility to shift emphasis/attack as appropriate (with management approval, of course).

The consultant's relationship with key managers below the level of top management will be important for success. He will need their cooperation and assistance, as well as their good will. Hence, various managers should be kept informed within the limits of necessary confidentiality. It would be well to avoid long closed-door sessions with the owner-manager, since such meetings tend to be threatening to those excluded.

Management supervision will be closest in a project assignment (one with a beginning, a middle and an end). A retainer consultant will normally be freer to investigate areas outside the original limits — again, always in concert with management. Most important, there should be communication on every visit, however brief. The door to top management must remain open. In the final analysis, the role of the consultant will be to recommend and, perhaps, assist with implementation. Management's role will be to make decisions, and this role cannot be delegated to any outside advisor, however competent or knowledgeable.

8

VALUING YOUR COMPANY

- ❏ Objectives
- ❏ Fundamentals of Small Company Valuation
- ❏ Dominant Factors
- ❏ Key Adjusting Factors
- ❏ Choosing Your Expert
- ❏ Valuing the Small Professional Firm
- ❏ Fair Market Value: Outside Purchaser
- ❏ Additional Value: Inside Owner-Manager

VALUING YOUR COMPANY

Objectives

There are many reasons why you might want to know the approximate value of your company. Among the most common are the following:

1. Proposed sale of the company or the acquisition of another.

2. Sale or issuance of company stock or the issuance of stock options.

3. Calculation of the transfer tax on the gift of company stock or for estate purposes.

4. Designing or updating a buy-sell agreement.

5. Determination of liquidity needs.

6. Partnership or corporation break-up or dissolution.

7. Marital dissolution.

8. Structuring multiple entities to allocate family wealth.

9. For any number of legal proceedings, such as breach of contract lawsuit.

In theory, there should be one "true" value for any company or, at least, one true narrow range of values. In practice, value is not only in the eye of the beholder, it can vary considerably with the objective(s) of the owner-manager. For example, in the sale or acquisition of a company, or in a court of law, the objective is usually "fair market value." This concept describes what a willing buyer would pay a willing seller in a free market, with both in possession of substantially all pertinent information, and neither under any compulsion or pressure to close such a transaction. Management might wish a low valuation on stock to be issued to key employees in order to make such stock affordable and, hence, maximize the incentive for extra effort. For a buy-sell agreement designed to protect survivors, a high valuation (funded by life insurance) might be sought. Be certain you know what your short- and long-term objectives are before you give any valuation expert the go-ahead. The purpose of this chapter, and the two case studies in Appendices A and B, is to help the reader to protect the company (and his or her equity in it) from being sacrificed on the altar of some half-baked ivory tower valuation process.

Fundamentals of Small Company Valuation

There are certain basic factors which are generally recognized by the professional appraisal community to be of particular importance in valuing any small, closely-held company. Most of these are spelled out in Internal Revenue Ruling 59-60, including the following:

1. Nature and history of the business.

2. General economic outlook, and the specific prospects for the industry.

3. Net worth and financial condition.

4. Earning capacity.

5. Dividend paying capacity.

6. Extent of goodwill, if any.

7. The size of the block of stock being valued, especially whether it represents a majority or minority interest.

8. Whether the stock in question is voting or non-voting.

9. Stock prices of comparable public companies.

10. Sale(s) of company stock at or near the valuation date.

11. Limitations or restrictions on the stock, such as transferability, dividends, etc.

12. Sale(s) of stock in comparable closely-held companies (implied.)

Exhibit 17 presents a list of questions which the author routinely submits to the owner/managers of a company to be valued. (This list would be also useful in conducting an in-depth analysis of the quality of the company for purely management

Exhibit 17

Valuation Data

1. Brief history of business
2. General outlook for this company
3. Primary customer base and outlook for *their* business
4. Simple organization chart
5. Resumes of key personnel, including owner
   a. length of service
   b. how critical
   c. salary, benefits
6. Proprietary nature of product(s) old and new, including:
   a. basic technology, trade secrets
   b. patents granted/pending/ applied for
   c. cost/performance relative to competition
7. Marketing
   a. channels
   b. sales force, including type, size, method of compensation
   c. advertising: extent and importance
8. Sales breakdown for fiscal year by:
   a. product or product line
   b. major customer(s)
   c. territory
9. Backlog by:
   a. product or product line
   b. major customer(s)
   c. territory
10. Historical projections of sales
11. Outlook for pricing of old and new products with reasons for any major projected changes

Exhibit 17 (continued)

12. Projections of sales for fiscal year
13. Competition
    a. major competitors, including size, financial strength
    b. nature of competition: technology, price, etc.
    c. company's position relative to competition:
       1) strengths
       2) weaknesses
14. Gross margins, especially any anticipated deterioration (reasons)
15. List of sole-sourced materials
16. Historical projections of profit and loss
17. P&L projections for next fiscal year
18. Any significant anticipated changes in financial conditions (reasons)
19. Banking relationship, including:
    a. loan officer
    b. credit availability
    c. loan agreements
    d. outstanding and anticipated debt
20. Any past sales of company stock
21. Any merger discussions
22. Publicly traded companies in same or similar business
23. Companies in this industry which have been acquired in the last three years
24. Existing or pending litigation
25. Any other information you consider pertinent to valuation at (date)

purposes, quite apart from valuation.) In fact, the principles are almost identical, because the value of the company is inevitably described by the strength of its operation as measured by the items on this list.

Dominant Factors

In a small company, four factors tend to dominate valuation; earning capacity, adjusted net worth, sale of company stock at or near the valuation date and market prices of truly comparable public companies. Earning capacity is probably the most important factor because it is the future after-tax earnings of the company which will almost always provide the return on investment for the buyer's purchase price. In this regard, historical earnings can be quite important, particularly if they can provide a reliable predictor of future performance. Credible projections, based upon historical earnings and a careful analysis of the nature and history of the business, as well as the economic outlook of the country and the industry, are essential in establishing a realistic projection of such a return on investment.

Adjusted net worth is simply book value per the company's balance sheet, adjusted for differences in asset values between that balance sheet and the market. Adjusted net worth is important because it provides a "floor" under risk, and is also an indicator of the quality of past financial management. While the sale of company stock in an arms-length transaction or the market price of a truly comparable public company would be excellent to have, they tend to be very unusual. In particular, a "truly comparable" public company is almost impossible to find. Companies sold in the public market are substantially larger and generally more diversified than small companies. The idea that one can usefully compare a $100 million company in a similar industry is, I believe, a fiction.

Key Adjusting Factors

Two key adjusting factors for the value of a small company are the discount for minority interest and the discount for lack of marketability. Any buyer of a minority interest in a privately held company will discount substantially from a proportionate value of 100% ownership of that company because he has little or no control. Even a substantial minority stockholder will often have little influence on company operations. Since privately held companies are much less marketable than the stocks of publicly held companies, this discount is also realistic and appropriate.

Choosing Your Expert

The art in valuing small companies is not in methodically walking through the IRS guidelines and/or data collection sheets, such as presented in Exhibit 17. Rather, it is in the selection from this mass of information those factors which are of telling importance in a particular case. Finding a valuation expert with a high level of competence in matters concerning small companies in general will be of great assistance in achieving the valuation results you are seeking. A case study assisting the reader to "walk through" a typical valuation process is presented in Appendix A.

Valuing the Small Professional Firm

The task of placing a precise value on a small professional firm, or portion thereof, is troublesome for any ethical expert. The expert's dilemma stems not so much from the supply of yardsticks provided by IRS, contending attorneys, or other experts; wending his or her way through such a thicket is part of the expert's stock in trade. Rather, the main problem is the disparity between the price an outsider would be willing to pay and the value to the active member of the firm. In each case, there is a willing buyer and a willing seller, both of whom are in possession of all material facts, and neither of whom is under any compulsion to close such a transaction. But when the seller is a spouse or departing partner, and the buyer is an owner-manager (rather than an outsider), "fair market value" can swing like a pendulum.

To an outsider, a small professional firm is little more than the people who operate it. It is axiomatic in valuing such firms that an acquirer is buying the people rather than the firm itself. The resulting dependence on a few key individuals creates risk, and the possibility that the owner-manager might well leave after being bought out serves to increase that risk, as does a modest backlog of business or a small proportion of repeat business.

While the outside purchaser would gain rights to a portion of the company's equity and any dividends were a purchase made, the insider owner-manager would retain control over salaries, bonuses, retirement plans, and other insider benefits. In addition, there would be a far greater likelihood of keeping the other key management and "production" personnel together as a team were the owner-manager to retain the ownership interest and buy out that of the spouse. Clearly, this approach yields a higher value than that which would be assigned by an outsider.

The primary objective of an impartial expert is to assist the parties in arriving at a value that is both reasonable and equitable. Hence, the opinion on the range of value should reflect both outside-purchaser *and* insider-value approaches. The former will typically suggest the "floor" of that range, and the latter, the "ceiling."

Fair Market Value: Outside Purchaser

The most commonly used basis for determining the acquisition price of a small professional firm is tangible net worth, or the net tangible assets less total liabilities. The reasons for this standard, utilized by a wide variety of professions in various parts of the country, all boil down to one fundamental and overriding consideration: dependence on a few key individuals. Since one or more of these persons can leave at virtually any time, there is no reliable way to predict future revenues or profits. Therefore, to pay substantially in excess of what the firm has compiled in net worth prior to the acquisition is to bank on a future return on investment that may not materialize. As a result, most acquisitions are based upon tangible net worth or, at least, a formula in which tangible net worth is weighted prominently among other factors. When assigning fair market value for an outside purchaser, the appraiser must, of course, carefully consider any recent sales of firm equity.

Additional Value: Insider Owner-Manager

Additional insider values can be measured in relation to specific financial benefits, as well as to the less tangible elements of control attendant to such ownership. A partial list of such factors would include salaries, bonuses, retirement plans, common executive perquisites (automobile, expense allowance, etc.), uncommon executive perquisites (apartment, extensive foreign travel, etc.), and control itself. This final item reflects the value (at least partially emotional) of retaining control of the firm as a whole, as opposed to control of individual aspects of firm operations. While intangible, the control premium can weigh very heavily on insider values.

The case study presented in Appendix B outlines the information considered and the conclusions reached by the author in a recent case involving a small professional firm, as well as the ultimate resolution of the case. While this case involved marital dissolution, the same basic principals would apply to other circumstances, such as a partnership breakup or sale of a partnership interest to a junior member of the firm.

A FINAL THOUGHT

A FINAL THOUGHT

Most of us in business know at least one small company manager who has gone through a divorce or has discovered that his children have grown up and he largely missed the process. Whatever success the manager has achieved in money, reputation, organization or contribution to the business community may seem hollow indeed in such circumstances. While each individual and family is unique, there is one preventive measure which seems to cut across all lines; namely, know your personal objectives and implement them through your business.

At the beginning of all long-term consulting associations, I make it a practice to initiate an extensive discussion concerning the personal objectives of the owner-manager(s) whom I will be advising. Typical questions would include:

What do you want to be doing five years from now, ten years from now; and where do you want to be doing it?

How important is money? Why is it important –
to live well, as a way of "keeping score", etc.?

How important are family considerations? How
old are your children? How important is the
quantity of time you spend with them? How
likely is this to change as they get older?

Do you enjoy business travel? Can you take
your spouse with you? Do you want to?

Do you have time for anything else besides
running the business and being with your family? Do you want to do other things? If not, how
will you spend your time when you retire?

After fifteen years of independent small
company management consulting, I am convinced
that accurate answers to such questions as these are
vital to the well being of the whole executive. Failure
to answer honestly, or not to bother to ask, significantly increases the chances that the business will
run the personal life, rather than the other way
around. The stresses on marital and parental relationships from such neglect are considerable.

This is not to suggest that personal planning
will somehow "wish away" the rigorous everyday
time and travel demands which nearly every small
company places on its management. Rather, it is to
underscore the simple truth that you are a person
first and an executive second. To allow professional
ego and single-minded ambition to undermine what

should be your major goals in life is to relinquish control over that life.

Plan now. Know where you want to go, and plot a course to get there. Don't look back in ten or fifteen years and wish you had done things differently. By then, it will be too late. You have the skill and foresight to plan the future of your business. Simply use the same skill and foresight to plan how that business will foster your personal goals and those of your family. The rewards for this kind of planning will be priceless.

Appendix A
CASE STUDY
VALUATION OF ABC RETAIL STORES, INC.

- ❑ $495 Per Share, As Per Stock Purchase Agreement
- ❑ Financial Condition
- ❑ Net Worth (Book Value)
- ❑ Corporate Earnings
- ❑ Sales
- ❑ Occupancy Costs
- ❑ Contingent Liabilities
- ❑ Earnings Potential
- ❑ Liquidation
- ❑ Discount for Minority Interest/Lack of Marketability
- ❑ Value Range
- ❑ Recommendation to the Parties

Appendix A

CASE STUDY
VALUATION OF ABC RETAIL STORES, INC.

Arriving at a fair and equitable valuation of a 40% interest in ABC Retail Stores, Inc. has been anything but an ordinary assignment. There is no shortage of useful and relevant information, most of which has been compiled in the same manner from month to month and year to year. The problem is that much of this information is inherently contradictory as to valuation issues.

For example, consider earnings. While the last two years have seen combined pre-tax losses for the corporation exceed $241,000, most of this period was without store #6, by far the most successful unit the corporation has ever operated. In addition, losses in store #5 have been cut substantially in recent months, from an average of over $23,000 per month in the first five months of the current year to around $9,000 per month over the last five months.

Sales, too, provide a mixed picture. While stores 3, 5, and 6 have shown good sales gains in

181

recent months, stores 2 and 4 have suffered significant losses, especially when inflation is taken into account.

The Stock Purchase Agreement provides some guidance; however, the fact that its stipulated value ($495 per share) has remained unchanged over a four-year period, despite a considerable increase in real market value, dilutes its impact.

It would seem evident that, if a valuation of $1,500,000 was correct in 1978, then the company is worth less than that today, owing to the sizeable losses and resulting deterioration of both the balance sheet and the company's short-term financial condition. On the other side of the ledger, however, most buyers look for return on investment as a primary yardstick for pegging a purchase price. Now that store #7 has been sold off and losses at store #5 are being brought under control, to say nothing of the rapid rise of store #6, the earnings future of the company appears much brighter today than it did even as recently as a year ago.

Finally, this company gives every indication of being the one company in a hundred whose liquidation value far exceeds its value as a going concern. The reason for this unusual situation is that, while each store could be run separately and profitably by a capable owner-manager, running all five requires an expensive overhead structure. As long as the company remains, in effect, "too small to be big and too big to be small," the sale of each store separately and the winding up of company affairs would likely yield far more to the stockholders than the sale of the corporation as a whole, with its present overhead structure remaining intact.

With such a welter of conflicting information, it is important to arrive at a methodology that makes the evidence more easily considered and understood by all parties. With this in mind, we shall employ a "straw man" valuation, and test that valuation with all important evidence available which might tend to make that valuation too high or too low. The value to be tested is as follows:

$495 Per Share, As Per
Stock Purchase Agreement

Let's take a look at the most important evidence on both sides of this value, first on the negative side.

Financial Condition

The financial condition of the company is not good at present, and has deteriorated considerably over the past two years. For example, the Current Ratio has dropped from 2:1 to 0.5:1. The Quick Ratio has dropped from 1:1 to near zero. Total Liabilities have gone from a position of equality with equity in 1979 to a 5:1 ratio in 1981. The Cash account showed a deficit of more than $70,000 at December 31, and Retained Earnings (the measure of the company's cumulative after-tax earnings from inception) is virtually zero. The company has a negative Working Capital in excess of $200,000.

In short, were it not for the significant rebound in earnings in recent months, and the solid prospects for earnings in the future, the company could most properly be considered in serious financial jeopardy, certainly not one which could command a price of anything like $1,500,000 in an arm's-length marketplace transaction.

Net Worth (Book Value)

Net Worth is often used as an important determinant in pegging a purchase price. It gives the buyer some feeling as to the underlying values in the company, as well as an idea of liquidation value should continuing to run the business prove unfeasible. Net Worth at December 31, 1981 was $145,682. Even a multiple on Book of two or three is far less than $1,500,000.

Corporate Earnings

Owning equally to operating losses at stores 5 and 7, and the size of corporate overhead, ABC Retail Stores, Inc. has been unprofitable as a company during three of the past four years. Without taking into consideration the gain on the sale of two stores, the company has sustained pre-tax losses of nearly $345,000 over the past two years, $300,000 of which was sustained in 1981. Even among the profitable units, the picture is not universally positive. Both stores 2 and 4 had sharply lower earnings in 1981 than in 1980 (down 30% and 50% respectively).

Sales

Sales for stores 2 and 4 are down considerably. Even when store 3 is included, sales for the three units combined are down slightly from 1981.

When these results are adjusted for inflation, the real drop in sales is more than 10%.

Occupancy Costs

Store #4 has had a cost-of-living rent increase as of March 1, 1981. Store #3 has one coming up on January 1.

Contingent Liabilities

The company is still in the position of guarantor of the lease at North Peninsula. Should the new owners fail, it is not unlikely that the company and/or its stockholders would be forced to find another tenant, and pay rent during the period of non-occupancy.

Now, let's look at the most important evidence on the positive side.

Earnings Potential

Now that the North Peninsula disaster is behind the company, only one losing unit is still on board, store #5, and with sales increasing, losses there have been reduced significantly. Even with store #5 losing over $50,000 during the first five months of calendar year 1981, the five current operating units showed earnings of more than $230,000.

If one assumes that pre-tax earnings in stores 2, 3, and 4 return to their 1980 levels, the earnings contribution of these three units would be $437,000. If we further assume that the current loss rate of $9,000 per month at store #5 is cut in half in 1982, that would translate into a year-end loss of $54,000.

Finally, store #6 should easily earn $250,000 itself this year.

Unfortunately, corporate overhead eats up these earnings and then some. If one assumes an overhead of $920,000 during 1982, the corporation as a whole would lose well over $230,000. It would take considerable cuts in corporate overhead and "perks" to get very far above break-even. The key positive point here is that the operating units as a group are quite profitable and could be very attractive sales vehicles if sold separately.

Liquidation

Since the sale of the individual units would yield a far higher sale price than could be realized from the sale of the company as a whole, it would be helpful to make certain assumptions regarding such a possible series of transactions.

1. Store #5 sold for just enough to pay off all its existing obligations.

2. Remaining four units sold separately, with buyers taking on all existing obligations.

3. Each buyer will require a first-year 20% after-tax return on investment (ROI) over and above any wages he might take out by replacing the existing manager. That ROI will be taken out as a year-end bonus, on which the buyer will pay 50% personal income taxes.

4. Each buyer will calculate first-year ROI on the earnings projected below:

Store #2

Projected Pre-tax Earnings (average 1980-1981)	$154,935
After-tax bonus ROI	$\dfrac{77,492}{.2} =$
Purchase Price (20% first-year ROI)	$387,458

Store #3

Projected Pre-tax Earnings (average 1980-1981)	$115,172
After-tax bonus ROI	$\dfrac{57,588}{.2} =$
Purchase Price (20% first-year ROI)	$287,932

Store #4

Projected Pre-tax Earnings (average 1980-1981)	$119,110
After-tax bonus ROI	$\dfrac{59,549}{.2} =$
Purchase Price (20% first-year ROI)	$297,744

Store #6

Projected Pre-tax Earnings (double the earnings from January 1980 through December 1981)	$257,858
After-tax bonus ROI	$\dfrac{128,940}{.2} =$
Purchase Price (20% first-year ROI)	$644,702

Total Net Sales Prices

Store #2	$387,458
Store #3	287,932
Store #4	297,744
Store #5	—
Store #6	644,702
Total	$1,617,836

The figure $1,617,836 represents, in my judgment, top dollar for these units sold separately. At that, the multiples on 1981 earnings for stores 2 and 4 are open to challenge as being far too high for units whose earnings dropped significantly from 1980.

Discount for Minority Interest/Lack of Marketability

It is important to remember that what is being valued here is not 40% of a sale price or group of sales prices, but rather a 40% interest in the stock of ABC Retail Stores, Inc. In other words, what would an outsider pay for a 40% interest in this company in an arm's-length transaction? Clearly, any informed buyer would want to discount substantially from $1,617,836 because of the lack of control. The fact that there is no ready market for these shares further reduces their value.

Such discounts typically range from 15-25%. In view of the strong vested interest of management in retaining the status quo, a discount of 20% is reasonable.

$$
\begin{array}{r}
\$1,617,836 \;\; \text{(pre-discount)} \\
\text{x } 80\% \\
\hline
\$1,294,269 \\
\text{x } 40\% \\
\hline
\$\;\; 517,708
\end{array}
$$

Value Range

After the above discount, a 40% interest in this company would be worth $517,708 – the top of the range, in my opinion. $350,000 would be the absolute floor, not only because of the liquidation values cited above, but because of the very high value to the buyer (management/remaining stockholders) of maintaining current salaries, benefits and freedom.

Recommendation to the Parties

That the value range be set at:
$350,000 to $517,708
and that negotiations proceed to determine the final sale price within this range, and the associated terms of sale.

Appendix B
CASE STUDY
VALUATION OF XYZ PROFESSIONAL FIRM

- ❑ Background

- ❑ Earnings

- ❑ Multiple on Earnings

- ❑ Tangible Net Worth

- ❑ Average of Two Values

- ❑ Additional Value/Inside Owner-Manager
    - ❑ Background
    - ❑ Pension Contributions as Bonus
        Earnings
    - ❑ Control Privileges

- ❑ Range of Values

- ❑ Outcome

Appendix B

CASE STUDY
VALUATION OF XYZ PROFESSIONAL FIRM

Background

In assessing the fair market value for an outsider, certain background factors are of importance, including the strength and reputation of the firm, the immediate outlook for business, the extent of over-concentration among the client base, the long-term business prospects, the financial strength of the firm, the degree of dependence on one or more key individuals, and the strength of competition.

XYZ has an outstanding professional reputation. The firm's philosophy has always been to hire the very best people available, and that insistence on quality is paying off. The immediate business outlook is clouded by the recession and by an apparent downturn ahead in business from the firm's principal client. While over-concentration played a major role in the firm's very high utilization percentage (and high profits) in fiscal year 1982, the loss of much of that business in 1983 will have a pronounced flattening effect on both revenues and profits.

Nevertheless, long-term prospects appear bright indeed. The need for expertise in the firm's strongest areas has grown in recent years, and there is every reason to expect that trend to continue. There seems little doubt as to the viability of the professional firm that can provide high quality services in this field. XYZ is well-positioned to take advantage of such future growth opportunities.

The financial condition of the company is exceptionally strong. There is virtually no debt at all. Well over two-thirds of the assets are Current Assets; that is, either cash or likely to turn into cash within one year. In fact, over one-half of total assets are Quick Assets, either cash or likely to turn into cash within 90 days. All important financial ratios are exemplary.

As is typical of the small professional firm, XYZ is extremely dependent on its three principals, not only for project management and technical expertise, but for generating business as well. This dependence is softened somewhat by the high incidence of repeat business from longtime clients. The fact that there are three key people at the top, rather than only one or two, is also helpful. But the vulnerability is there nonetheless, and it inevitably influences the value of the firm.

Competition in this field is stiff, and it includes some of the largest and most prestigious firms in the country. However, of all the obstacles in the firm's path to continued growth and prosperity, competition from the giants should be among the easiest to handle. Surely, it has proven to be up to now. So long as the firm maintains a deserved reputation for quality services, management should be able to concentrate on developing client relationships, rather than on reacting to its competitors.

Earnings

The recent earnings history of the firm is excellent. Exhibit 18 displays this history, with results restructured to show earnings before discretionary expenses. During this period, Net Revenues increased at an annual rate of 39%; Gross Margin, 42%; Operating Income, 61%; and Profit Before Discretionary Expenses, 69%. Pension Contributions increased eightfold and bonuses and deferred salaries, sevenfold. Even when compared with the excellent year of 1981, fiscal year 1982 showed increases in these categories of 28%, 27%, 45%, 51%, and 18%, respectively.

Were the husband to leave the firm and join (in a comparable position) a large competitor, his compensations would probably be approximately the same as his current salary (base and deferred): $150,000. Based upon this information, Exhibit 19 displays restated earnings for XYZ, after adding back management bonuses, including appropriate rates of federal and state (deductible) income taxes. This exhibit assumes that partner #1 could also command $150,000 in another firm, and that partner #2 would get $100,000. Other professional bonuses are disregarded.

Most professional firms would covet such an earnings history. Moreover, despite the above cave-

Exhibit 18

Pretax Profitability: FY 1982, 1981, 1980

(In Thousands)

	1982	**1981**	**1980**
Sales	$3,540	$2,777	$1,830
Direct Expenses[1]	1,785	1,343	930
Project Expenses	140	156	98
Gross Margin	1,615	1,278	802
Overhead	380	428	325
Operating Income	1,235	850	477
Other Income (Exp.)[2]	75	17	(18)
Profit Before Discretionary Expenses and Taxes	1,310	867	459
Bonuses/Deferred Salary	865	773	127
Pension Expense	188	74	23
Profit Before Taxes	$ 257	$ 60	$ 309

[1]Excludes pension expense and profit sharing.
[2]Excludes federal and state income taxes.

Exhibit 19

Restated Profitability: FY 1982, 1981, 1980

(In Thousands)

	1982	1981	1980
Pretax Profit Per Exhibit[1]	$257	$ 60	$309
Add Back Bonuses[1]	408[2]	213[3]	—[4]
Restated Pretax Profit	$665	$273	$309
Federal Income Tax	288	77	94
State Income Tax[5]	34	14	16
Profit After Taxes (Restated)	$343	$182	$199

[1]Assumes comparable compensation for three principles in other firms at $150,000, $150,000, and 100,000, respectively, totaling $400,000.

[2]Entire bonus for all three principals added back.

[3]Represents total salary and bonus for the three principals, less $400,000.

[4]Total compensation for each principal below comparable per footnote #1 above.

[5]Assumes state income tax is deductible (46%) for computation of federal tax.

ats regarding near-term business prospects, there is every reason to believe that the firm's historical results are a reliable indicator of its long-term earning capacity. The growing need for such services, together with the skills and reputation of the firm and its key personnel, points to a future of continued growth in revenues and profits.

Multiple on Earnings

A commonly employed yardstick for arriving at the value of a company is a "multiple" on earnings; that is, a number by which historical (or projected, if available) after-tax earnings are multiplied. The buyer's confidence that fast-growth historical earnings are, in fact, a reliable predictor of future earning capacity is the key ingredient in determining the multiple. The higher the confidence that earnings will continue to grow at a fast rate, the higher the multiple. The greater the uncertainty, the lower the multiple and the more the buyer would tend to look to underlying balance sheet values in establishing the offer.

Multiples are normally applied either to the most recent fiscal year's earnings or to a weighted average of the most recent three-to-five years earnings. Since the growth in profitability has been very dramatic since 1980, and the immediate future could be flat or down somewhat, a multiple on weighted average earnings is the most sensible in this case. Experience shows that multiples on the earnings of service companies in general and professional firms in particular, are well below those of industry. A range of 4-6 on the most recent year is typical. Hence, a multiple of 4 on a weighted average of the most recent three fiscal years is most reasonable, in the opinion of the appraiser. Employing weights of 1, 2, and 3 for fiscal years 1980, 1981, and 1982, a multiple of 4 on the three-year weighted average earnings of $264,000 suggests a value of $1,056,000.

In testing the appropriateness of a 4 multiple in this situation, one discovers that the value derived is approximately 5% greater than the present value of $264,000 per year for five years, using a discount rate of 10%, and assuming that the base earnings figure will keep pace with inflation. Since a five-year outsider's "window" is itself most appropriate for a small, highly successful professional firm, the 4 multiple on weighted average earnings seems quite reasonable.

Tangible Net Worth

"Tangible Net Worth" begins with the company's book value (also called net asset value, net worth, or stockholders' equity) and adjusts that balance sheet figure to reflect differences between the market value of certain assets and their depreciated value on the books. This method is especially helpful in cases in which the buyer's window to the future is short-term, cloudy, or both. It is the rare small professional firm for which adjusted book value fails to play a major role in determining fair market value.

Total stockholders' equity at February 28, 1982 was $760,000. From this total must be subtracted $95,000 of doubtful Accounts Receivable.

On the other side of the ledger, certain fixed assets have been depreciated below market value. Appropriate asset value adjustments are shown in Exhibit 20 together with the calculation of adjusted book value.

The most recent stock sale occurred in this firm when partner #3 purchased equity for 125% of tangible net worth. While it might be argued that partner #3 was paying a premium for insider status his position as a minority stockholder undercuts that argument. In other words, a 25% premium over tangible net worth at that time was deemed reasonable by both buyer and seller and, given the firm's current standing in the profession, would appear appropriate today, especially for the majority interest in question here. Thus, 125% of the tangible net worth shown in Exhibit 20 is $860,000.

Average of Two Values

One must always be cautious of relying on a single method for determining the value of any company, particularly a small professional firm. While an average of two common methods is not perfect, such a procedure sharply reduces the risk of arriving at a value or value range that is unreasonable. The average value derived from the two methods above (4 times weighted average earnings and 125% of adjusted book value) is $958,000. In my opinion, this sum represents the fair market value a prospective outside buyer would pay for XYZ professional firm. Such a buyer would likewise, pay a proportionate amount for the community's 60% interest: namely, $575,000.

Exhibit 20
Adjusted Asset Values/Adjusted Book Value

	Net Book Value	Estimated Market Value
Auto #1[1]	$ 300	$ 7,000
Auto #2[1]	2,400	8,000
Auto #3[1]	4,600	10,000
Leasehold Improvements[2]	1,500	6,800
Total	$8,800	$ 31,800

Total Difference $23,000	
Book Value (Stockholder's Equity) per balance sheet	$760,000
Less Accounts Receivable Adjustment	(95,000)
Plus Depreciated Asset Value Adjustment	23,000
Adjusted Book Value	$688,000
× 125% = $860,000	

[1]Estimates on automobiles from Bay Area dealerships.

[2]Based upon straight-line depreciation over the five-year lease term.

APPENDIX B

Additional Value: Inside
Owner-Manager

Background

While an outsider purchasing the commu-
nity's interest in this firm would, in my opinion, pay
approximately $575,000, such interest is far more
valuable to an owner-manager retaining this level of
ownership. Additional insider values can be measured in relation to specific financial benefits, as well
as to the less tangible elements of control attendant
to such ownership. The two most important financial benefits associated with ownership-manage-
ment in this firm are bonuses and participation in
the pension plan.

In the last three fiscal years, the husband
earned bonuses of $20,000, $73,000, and $54,000,
respectively, for a weighted average of $54,667
($27,333 after taxes). In the context of insider
benefits, there is a higher value associated with
bonuses than holds as part of restated earnings.
First, the owner-manager retains control over this
benefit and, second, there is a higher level of confidence that historical bonuses will be maintained
because the team is staying together. Whereas an
outsider with a five-year window would quite properly set a multiple of 4 on management bonuses (as
part of restated earnings), an insider could conser-
vatively increase that multiple to 5, thereby adding
insider value of $27,333.

Pension Contributions
as Bonus Earnings

The pension plan provides a firm contribution of up to 15% of an employee's compensation. Such contributions avoid taxation until withdrawn in retirement when, presumably, one's tax bracket will be lower. Since another firm employing the husband would doubtless have a similar plan, the relevant amount upon which to base added insider value from the pension plan is, again, the bonus. Fifteen percent of $54,667 is $8,200. The present value of $8,200 contributed annually to the pension fund for seven years, at a discount rate of 10%, is $39,921. For purposes of this analysis, it is assumed that whatever income taxation there is at retirement will be balanced by the two major imponderables associated with any retirement plan:

1. Compound earnings generated over decades on that portion of fund contributions and profits that would have gone for federal and state income taxes had the participant chosen instead to take out the $8,200 in added current compensation.
2. Proportional increases in fund participation by those staying with the firm upon the departure of employees not fully vested in the fund.

Thus, pension contributions on bonus earnings add insider value of $39,921.

Control Privileges

Beyond the hard numbers discussed above, assigning a value to such things as control over bonuses and pension contributions, determination of the kind of company car to purchase for oneself, etc., becomes very difficult and subjective. Just being able to run one's own firm ought to be worth something. But just how much? Clearly, any manager would gladly pay an additional $10,000 for the privileges associated with control. But is it worth $100,000? Probably not. Fifty thousand dollars, though arguable, seems reasonable in this case.

Range of Values

In my opinion, the value of the community's 60% interest in XYZ Professional Firm ranges from $575,000 to $692,000. (See Exhibit 21.) I recommend that the parties accept this range, and proceed to seek a mediated settlement figure within it.

Outcome

After a modest downward revision of the suggested range of values, pursuant to specific concerns raised by the husband, a series of negotiations (conducted by the respective counsel) followed. These negotiations included, predictably, support payments and other issues, as well as the firm's value, and were successfully concluded after a number of months. The negotiated firm value was within the final range suggested by the appraiser.

Exhibit 21

Fair Market Value
Inside Owner-Manager

Fair Market Value:	
Outside Purchaser	$575,000
Additional Bonus Value	27,333
Bonus-Related Pension	
Plan Value	39,921
Control Premium	50,000
Total Value	$692,254

INDEX

INDEX

INDEX

ORDER FORM
Lomas Publishing Co.
625 Ellis Street, Suite 301
Mountain View, CA 94043 USA

Please send me

_____ copies of BIG PROFITS FROM SMALL
COMPANIES (Hardcover)

@ $19.95 each $ _____ . __

Sales tax: Californians add $1.20/book   _____ . __

and/or

_____ copies of BIG PROFITS FROM SMALL
COMPANIES (Softcover)

@ $12.95 each   _____ . __

Sales tax: Californians add $.78/book   _____ . __

Shipping: $1.00 for the first book,
25¢ each additional book   _____ . __

_____ I can't wait 3-4 weeks for
Book Rate. Here is $2.50/ book
for Airmail.   _____ . __

Total of Check Enclosed $ _____ . __

I understand that I may return this book for a full
refund within 30 days of receipt if I am not completely
satisfied.

Name: _____

Address: _____

_____

_____ Zip: _____

ORDER FORM
Lomas Publishing Co.
625 Ellis Street, Suite 301
Mountain View, CA 94043 USA

Please send me

_____ copies of BIG PROFITS FROM SMALL
COMPANIES (Hardcover)
@ $19.95 each $ _____ . _____
Sales tax: Californians add $1.20/book   _____ . _____

and/or

_____ copies of BIG PROFITS FROM SMALL
COMPANIES (Softcover)
@ $12.95 each   _____ . _____
Sales tax: Californians add $.78/book   _____ . _____
Shipping: $1.00 for the first book,
25¢ each additional book   _____ . _____

_____ I can't wait 3-4 weeks for
Book Rate. Here is $2.50/ book
for Airmail.   _____ . _____

Total of Check Enclosed $ _____ . _____

I understand that I may return this book for a full
refund within 30 days of receipt if I am not completely
satisfied.

Name: _____

Address: _____

_____

_____ Zip: _____